Time Value of Money

A Key to Finance

Yu Peng Lin

Texas A&M University–Kingsville

Kendall Hunt
publishing company

Kendall Hunt
publishing company

www.kendallhunt.com
Send all inquiries to:
4050 Westmark Drive
Dubuque, IA 52004-1840

ISBN 978-0-7575-7676-8

Printed in the United States of America
10 9 8 7 6 5 4 3 2 1

To WeiJu, Ethan, and Pelon

Contents

Introduction

A key concept as it is, *time value of money* has not been extensively introduced in most of the finance textbooks we encountered. In our experience, students who understand the intuition underlying the basic but crucial concepts are better able to develop the critical judgment necessary in real-world decision-making situations. The ultimate goal of this book is to help students succeed in the classroom and to retain the concept they learned afterward. Our book offers a level of rigor that is appropriate for finance/business majors but presents the content in a manner that both majors and non-majors find accessible and practical.

Consider the following question: You are planning to buy a house in 5 years. You plan to give \$60,000 as the down payment. How much should you save/invest each month/year from now to achieve this goal? Or in a long-run version of the question: You plan to retire in 20 years. After careful assessment of the living expenses and life expectancy after retirement, you figure you will need \$600,000 upon retirement. How much should you save/invest each month/year to attain this goal? These are common, daily life questions that reveal a key concept in the field of finance—the *time value of money.*

In the most general sense, *time value of money* refers to the simple concept that a dollar in hand today is worth more than a dollar promised at some time in the future. Practically, one reason for this is that you could earn interest while you waited; so, a dollar today would *grow* to more than a dollar years later. How much it could grow depends on the interest rate you can earn in saving/investing. Now, turn back to the previous questions. Clearly, it is not necessary to save \$12,000 a year (\$60,000/5) or \$1,000 a month (\$60,000/60) to achieve the \$60,000 down payment unless there you are receiving zero interest. Assuming a positive interest rate, the figures should be somewhat lower. The same concept applies to the second version of the question. Money grows over time assuming it is invested with a positive interest rate. Thus, the further in the future you receive a dollar, the less it is worth today.

Economically, the notion of time value of money impacts various aspects of decision-making. The tradeoff between money today and money at some future date depends in part on the rate of interest you can earn. Thus, the higher the interest rate, the most likely it is that people will elect to save/invest and forego current consumption (unless it is necessary). Hence, in an economic sense, interest rate is considered the *opportunity cost* of spending money. Clearly, the higher the interest rate, the more your savings/investment will earn and the higher will be the opportunity cost of your spending.

Chapter 1
Future Value

We will start from the most straightforward concept—future value. *Future value* (FV) refers to the total amount of money a saving/investment will achieve over some periods of time at a given interest rate. Put it simply, *future value* is the value of a saving/investment at some point in the future. Drawing a timeline will usually help one see what is occurring.

Figure 1.1 shows the FV as how much an investment will be worth *n* periods from now. The investment today is clearly the \$, cash flow as we call it. The most important thing is that we write down the cash flows where they actually occur. In Figure 1.1, the cash flow occurs today, which we label as Time 0. We therefore put \$ at Time 0 on the timeline. Let's start out by considering the simplest case—single cash flow.

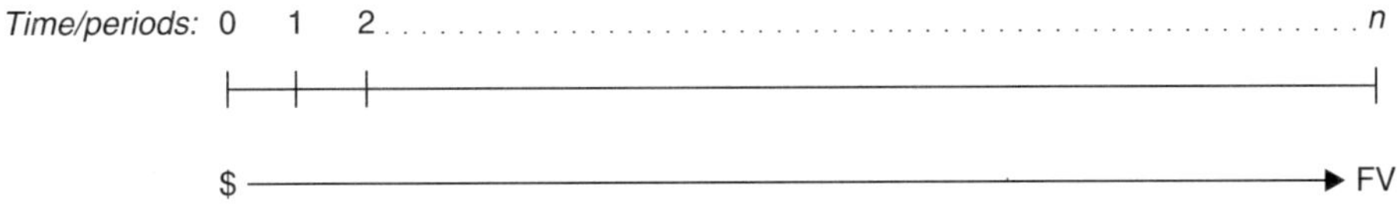

Figure 1.1 The timeline of future value

1.1: Single Cash Flow

We define *single cash flow* in the context of FV as there being **only one** deposit/investment that has been made. No further deposits/investments are allowed in the meantime. Consider, for instance, you were to deposit \$1,000 in a savings account that pays 10% annual interest rate. How much would you have in 1 year? Obviously, you would have \$1,100, which is the original principal of \$1,000 plus \$100 in interest that you earn over 1 year. We call \$1,100 the FV of \$1,000 deposited today for 1 year at 10%. In other words, we interpret that \$1,000 today is worth \$1,100 a year later assuming a 10% interest rate. A timeline can be shown as follows in Figure 1.2.

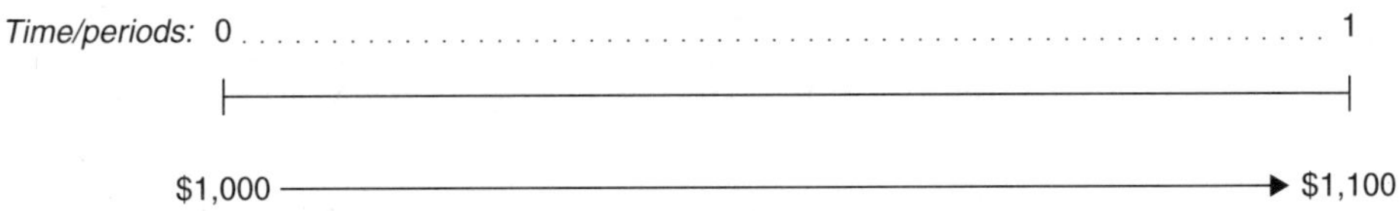

Figure 1.2 The future value of \$1,000 over 1 year at 10%

$$FV = \text{Original Principal} \times (1 + i) \quad \textbf{(1A)}$$

where

i = interest rate per period

Hence, following Equation (1A), the FV of $1,000 deposited with 10% annual interest rate in 1 year is 1000 × (1 + 10%) = 1,100.

Note that Equation (1A) is not a complete form since we only consider one period. Now, let's examine a slightly more demanding but complete version of the example: You were to deposit $1,000 in a savings account that pays 10% annual interest rate. How much would you have in 2 years? Certainly, it is necessary to assume that there are no further deposits or withdraws in the meantime. The answer, clearly, is $1,210, which is the summation of the original principal of $1,000 and $210 in interest earned. But wait a second! Shouldn't the interest earned be only $200 because there is 10% annual interest rate on the original principal of $1,000 for 2 years? This is a sound observation but incomplete. Figure 1.3 shows exactly what is occurring.

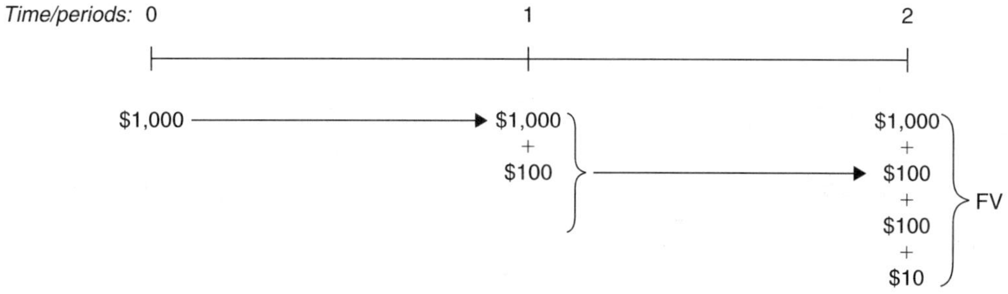

Figure 1.3 Future value of $1,000 over 2 years at 10%

In the first year, you would have $1,100 in the account. Then the whole amount of $1,100 rolls over for another year. Hence, the 10% annual interest in the second year applied not only to the original principal of $1,000 but also to the interest of $100 earned in the first year. As a result, the interest earned in the second year would be $100 (on the original principal) plus $10 (on the first year's interest). Summing up, we have $1,210 as the FV over 2 years. The process in which interest earned in previous periods gains interest in the following periods is called *compounding,* which means earning *interest on interest*. The opposite is called *simple interest,* in which the interest rate applies only to the original principal, not to the interest earned previously. Hence, with simple interest, the FV would have been only $1,200.

Therefore, a more complete Equation with the compounding feature is:

$$FV_n = \text{Original Principal} \times (1 + i)^n \quad \textbf{(1B)}$$

where n is the number of compounding periods, which is the length of time the deposit stays in the account, and i is the interest rate per compounding interval.

Following Equation (1B), the FV of a $1,000 deposit with 10% annual interest rate in 2 years is $1000 \times (1 + 10\%)^2 = 1{,}210$.

Challenge Questions

John deposits \$2,000 in a banking account today and plan to hold it there for 10 years.

A. Assume 5% annual interest rate: how much would he have over 10 years?

B. Assume 10% annual interest rate: how much would he have over 10 years?

A much easier way of computing FV in Equation (1B) is to use the interest factor table in Appendix B. Specifically, the element of $(1 + i)^n$ in Equation (1B) is called the future value interest factor ($FVIF_i^n$), where i is the interest rate per compounding period and n is the number of compounding periods. Hence, Equation (1B) can be rewritten as:

$$FV_n = \text{Original Principal} \times (1 + i)^n.$$
$$= \text{Original Principal} \times FVIF_i^n \qquad \textbf{(1B')}$$

Besides time, the interest rate is the major determinant of the FV. Thus, as shown in Figure 1.4, the higher the interest rate, the faster the money will grow. Moreover, the effect of compounding is not great over short time periods. However, it really starts to add up as the horizon grows.

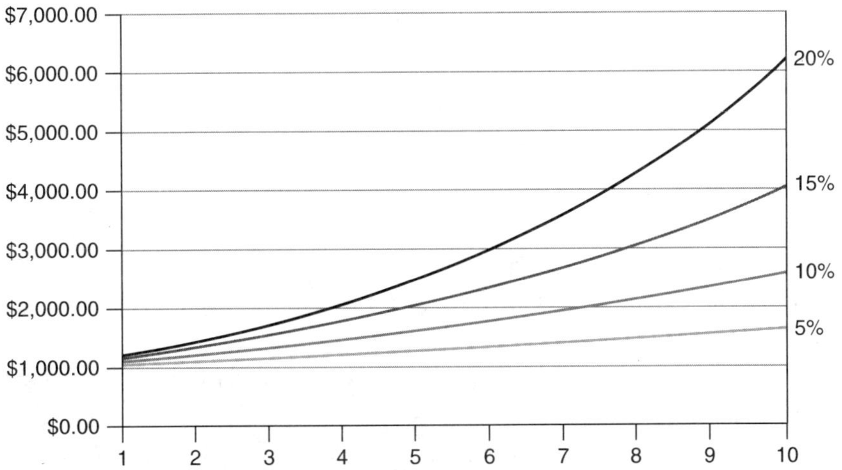

Figure 1.4 A \$1,000 deposit over 10 years with various interest rates

1.2: Multiple Cash Flows

A more complex and yet more practical case is the FV of multiple cash flows. Multiple cash flows can be simply defined as having more than one deposit/investment over time, as shown in Figure 1.5.

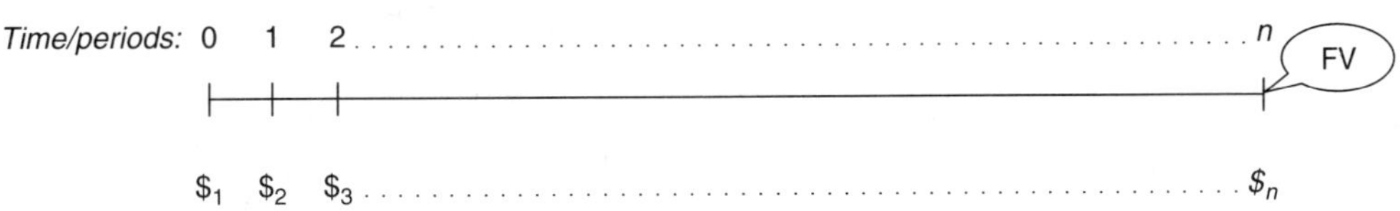

Figure 1.5 Timeline of multiple cash flows

The multiple cash flows are shown as the series of \$s ($\$_1, \$_2, \$_3, \ldots\ldots, \$_n$). The FV of interest is at the end of n periods. For instance, you could arrange to deposit \$1,000, \$900, \$500, \$1,100, \$400, and \$600 in a savings account for the following 5 years starting now. How much would you have over 5 years assuming 10% annual interest rate? Unfortunately, without further assumptions, the FV of multiple cash flows (the Grand FV) can only be found as the summation of the FVs of each corresponding cash flow, as shown in Figure 1.6.

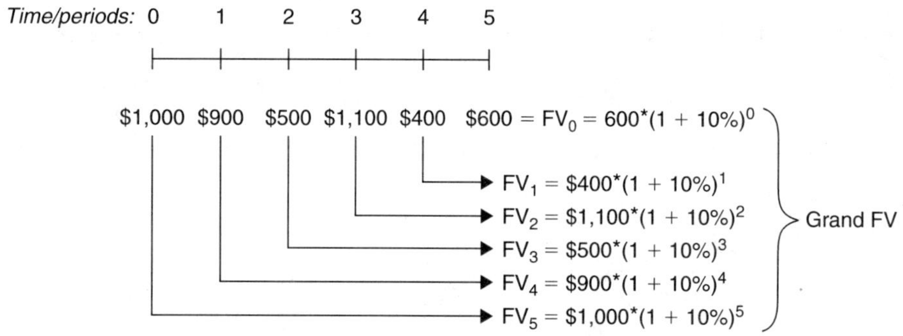

Figure 1.6 Future value of multiple cash flows

Hence,

$$\begin{aligned}
&\textit{The Future Value of Multiple Cash Flows (the Grand FV)}\\
&= FV_0 + FV_1 + FV_2 + FV_3 + FV_4 + FV_5\\
&= 600 \times (1 + 10\%)^0 + 400 \times (1 + 10\%)^1 + 1100 \times (1 + 10\%)^2\\
&\quad + 500 \times (1 + 10\%)^3 + 900 \times (1 + 10\%)^4 + 1000 \times (1 + 10\%)^5\\
&= 5{,}964.70
\end{aligned}$$

Note that the compounding period varies over each cash flow. It depends on how long a certain cash flow stays in the account. For instance, since the first deposit—\$1,000 occurs today, it stays in the account for 5 full years. Therefore, the compounding period on the first deposit is 5 years. The last cash flow of \$600 is deposited at the very end of the timeline; hence, it does not have the chance to compound yet which leads to a compounding period of 0.

Generally, we can draw a timeline of multiple cash flows and show the grand FV as in Figure 1.7.

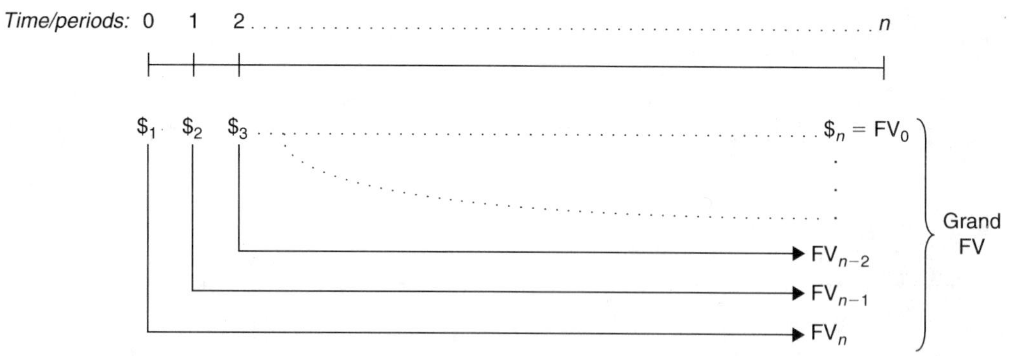

Figure 1.7 Timeline of multiple cash flows

The Future Value of Multiple Cash Flows

$$= FV_0 + FV_1 + FV_2 + \dots\dots + FV_n$$
$$= \$_n \times (1+i)^0 + \$_{n-1} \times (1+i)^1 + \dots\dots + \$_1 \times (1+i)^n \quad \textbf{(1C)}$$

Challenge Question

C. Eddie deposits $1,000 today, $500 in year 1, and $900 in year 2 in an account with 8% annual interest rate. He plans to hold all the deposits in the account for 5 years. How much would Eddie have at the end of 5 years?

1.3: Complications

In practice, most of banking accounts compound *monthly*. To find the FV of a deposit that compounds other than annually, we need to modify Equation (1B). Consider, for instance, Mark deposits $1,000 in an account with 12% annual interest rate. The account compounds monthly. How much would Mark have over a year? Clearly, the deposit compounds 12 times over a year. Hence, the compounding period would be 12 which is the n in Equation (1B). However, we also need to transform the annual interest rate to a monthly interest rate. This can be done simply by dividing the annual interest rate (12%) by 12 (month). Hence, the interest rate (i) in Equation (1B) would be 1%. Formally,

$$\begin{aligned} FV_{12} &= 1{,}000 \times \left(1 + \frac{12\%}{12}\right)^{12} \\ &= 1{,}000 \times FVIF_{1\%}^{12} \\ &= 1{,}126.80 \end{aligned}$$

Generally, we use the following Equation to calculate FV with various compounding intervals.

$$\begin{aligned} FV_{m\times n} &= \$ \times \left(1 + \frac{i}{m}\right)^{m\times n} \\ &= \$ \times FVIF_{i/m}^{m\times n} \end{aligned} \quad \textbf{(1D)}$$

where

i = annual interest rate
n = number of years
m = number of times per year that the account compounds

Recall that compounding confers interest on interest. Hence, more frequent compounding leads to more interest on interest. In the current example, since the account Mark holds compounds 12 times a year, he would expect to earn more interest than 12%. In other words, investing in this account would earn him a rate of return higher than the account's annual interest rate (i.e. 12%). A basic rate of return—*Effective Annual Rate (EAR)* shows this crucial idea.

$$\text{EAR} = \frac{\text{Ending Balance over a year} - \text{Beginning Balance}}{\text{Beginning Balance}} \times 100\% \qquad \textbf{(1E)}$$

EAR is merely the annual rate of return incorporates the compounding feature of the account. Following Equation (1E), the EAR of the account is 12.68%. Note that the EAR is higher than the quoted interest rate on the account (12%). It is due to the very simple fact that the account compounds 12 times a year. Consequently, the account earns more than 12%. In fact, as long as an account compounds more than once in a year, the EAR is generally higher than the quoted annual interest rate.

Challenge Questions

D. Mary deposits $1,000 today in an account with 8% annual interest rate. Assume the account compounds quarterly. How much would Mary have at the end of 2 years? What is the EAR of the account?

E. Sarah deposits $2,000 today, $1,500 in year 1, and $900 in year 2 in an account with 12% annual interest rate. Assume the account compounds monthly. She plans to hold all the deposits in the account for 5 years. How much would Sarah have at the end of 5 years?

Chapter 2
Present Value

A more complex but more practical concept is *present value* (PV). PV is the current worth of a future sum of money at a given interest rate. The interest rate used is generally referred to as the *discount rate.* In other words, PV is the value today of an amount of money in the future. The concept of PV is very useful because it tells us the required amount of a deposit/investment today to achieve at a targeted amount in the future at a given interest rate. Consider, for instance, you are planning to buy a flat panel TV in 1 year. The price is $1,100. How much would you deposit in an account with 10% interest rate today that will achieve $1,100 a year later? The answer is $1,000. This simple example illustrates the general truth that the PV of a future amount is less than the actual future amount.

Figure 2.1 shows the timeline of a PV. The PV is the current worth of a future amount of money. We put down the cash flows where they occur. Note that the PV is in fact the *original principal* and $ is actually the FV in the context of FV (see Figure 1.1). Hence, calculating PV is only a methodological reversal of computing FV. Let's start out by considering the simplest case—single cash flow.

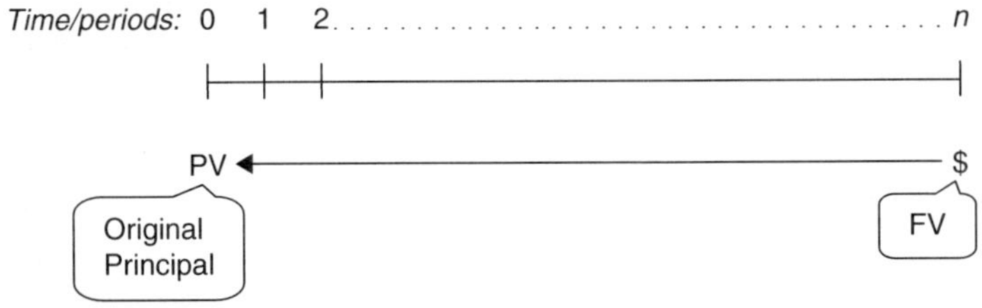

Figure 2.1 Timeline of a present value

2.1: Single Cash Flow

As defined in Section 1.1, *single cash flow* refers to the fact that **only one** cash flow that has been made. No further cash flows are allowed in the meantime. Let's revisit the previous example of purchasing a flat panel TV. You need $1,100 a year after for the TV. Hence, a simple timeline can be drawn as shown in Figure 2.2.

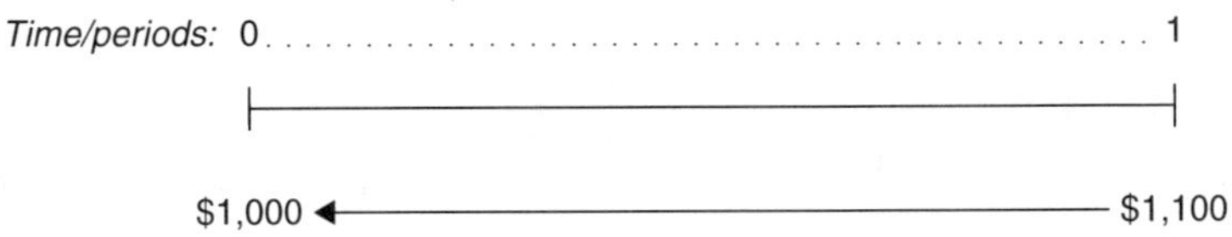

Figure 2.2 Present value of $1,100 at 10%

The PV of \$1,100 a year after is therefore \$1,000. In the current example, \$1,000 is the necessary amount of deposit/investment today to achieve \$1,100 a year later at 10% interest rate. One interpretation is that you need to deposit and remain \$1,000 in the account with 10% interest rate and it will yield \$1,100 a year later. Needless to say, no further deposits or withdraws are allowed in the meantime. The process of deriving PV is usually called *discounting,* which is just opposite *compounding.* In other words, discounting simply means *de-interest*—taking out the interest. Because we are trying to find the value today (PV) which is not yet *going through time*, there is no reason to assume interest.

Discounting is merely a methodological reversal of compounding. It is relatively easier to lay out the question in the context of FV first and solve for the unknown (PV in this case). Hence, following Equation (1A), we have

$$FV = PV \times (1 + i)$$

Hence,

$$PV = \frac{FV}{(1 + i)} \qquad \textbf{(2A)}$$

where

i = interest rate per period.

Hence, following Equation (2A), the PV of \$1,100 a year after is $\frac{1{,}100}{(1 + 10\%)} = 1{,}000$

Note that Equation (2A) is not complete because we consider only one period. Now, let's examine a slightly more demanding but complete version of the example. Assume you are actually planning to buy a TV in 2 years, not 1 year. Now, how much would you need to have in the account today? Intuitively, the amount should be less than \$1,000 because there in more interest involved in 2 years (Figure 2.3).

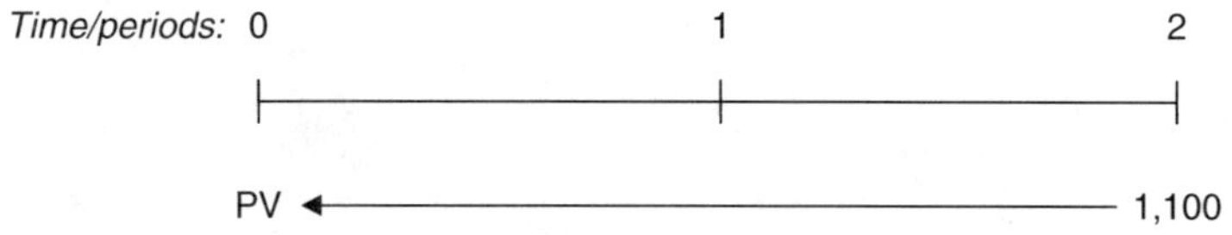

Figure 2.3 Present value of \$1,100 over 20 years at 10%

Following the FV Equation (1B), we have

$$FV_n = PV \times (1 + i)^n.$$

where

n = 2 in the current example.

Hence,

$$1{,}100 = PV \times (1 + 10\%)^2$$

$$PV = \frac{1{,}100}{(1 + 10\%)^2} = 909.09$$

Hence, you need to deposit \$909.09 in the account today.

In turn, a more general and complete Equation for PV is as follows.

$$PV = \frac{FV_n}{(1+i)^n} \tag{2B}$$

A much easier way of computing PV in Equation (2B) is to use the interest factor table in Appendix C. Specifically, Equation (2B) can be further rewritten as

$$\begin{aligned} PV &= \frac{FV_n}{(1+i)^n} \\ &= FV_n \times \frac{1}{(1+i)^n} \\ &= FV_n \times PVIF_i^n \end{aligned} \tag{2B'}$$

The element of $\frac{1}{(1+i)^n}$ in Equation (2B') is called the present value interest factor ($PVIF_i^n$) where i is the interest rate per period and n is the discounting period.

Challenge Question

F. Sue is planning her retirement 15 years from now. She figures she will need \$500,000 at retirement. Assume she could deposit at an account that guarantees her 6% annual interest rate. How much would she deposit today as a lump sum to achieve that goal?

Finally, the two major determinants of PV are *discount rate* and *time*. As shown in Figure 2.4, to arrive at \$1,000 in 10 years, the higher the discount rate, the lower is the required initial deposit. At the same rate, the longer the horizon, the lower is the necessary deposit today.

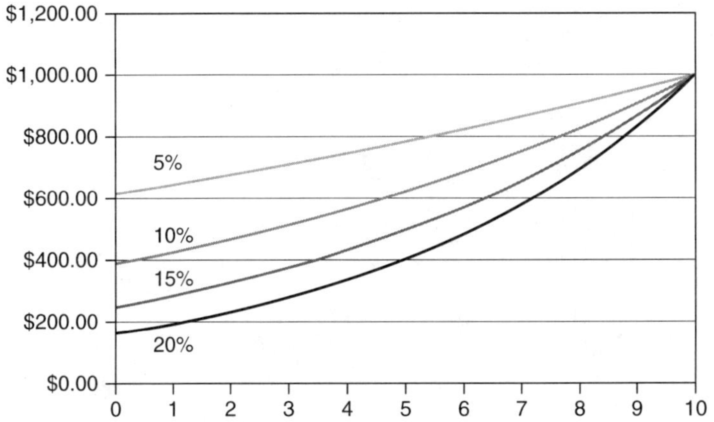

Figure 2.4 Present value of \$1,000 over 10 years with various discount rates

2.2: Multiple Cash Flows

Now we turn to a more complex situation. You are considering a possible investment opportunity of 3 years. The investment will yield \$1,000 in the first year, \$5,000 in year 2, and \$3,000 in year 3. How much is this investment worth today assuming a 15% discount rate?

To determine the PV of multiple cash flows, it is important to determine the timing of the expected cash flows. A cash flow timeline, like the one shown in Figure 2.5, illustrates when the cash flows are expected to occur and assists in determining the PV of the expected cash flows. Time 0 is today and is used to identify the current worth of the investment.

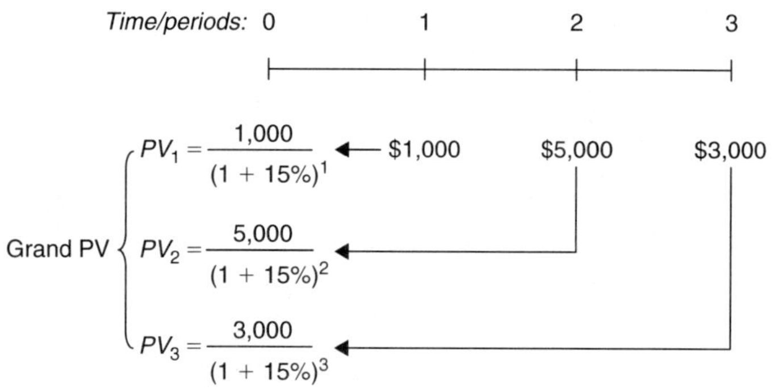

Figure 2.5 Present value of multiple cash flows

At the current example, there is no shortcut in computing the overall PV of the investment (grand PV) other than to calculate and sum up the PVs on each expected future cash flow. Hence, the grand PV is:

$$\begin{aligned}\textit{The PV of Multiple Cash Flows (Grand PV)} &= \frac{1,000}{(1+15\%)^1} + \frac{5,000}{(1+15\%)^2} + \frac{3,000}{(1+15\%)^3} \\ &= 6,622.83\end{aligned}$$

This means that the **current worth** of the investment is \$6,622.83. Most important, it could be interpreted that you would be willing to pay \$6,622.83 today for the cash flows mentioned above. In other words, if such an investment opportunity does exist, the fair value of it is \$6,622.83 at a 15% interest rate.

Extending the previous example to n periods leads to a more general timeline (Figure 2.6).

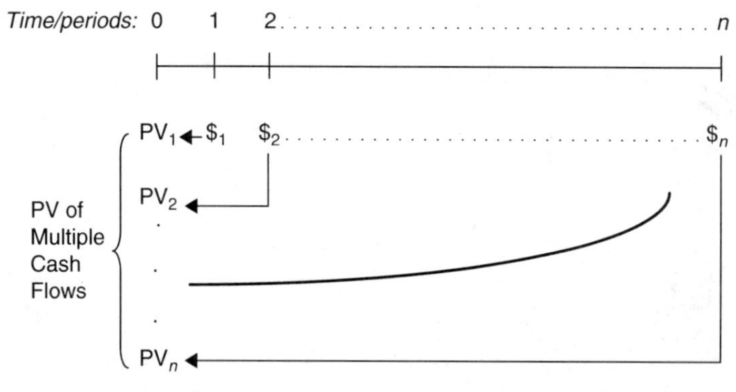

Figure 2.6 Present value of multiple cash flows

The PV of Multiple Cash Flows

$$= PV_1 + PV_2 + \ldots\ldots\ldots\ldots + PV_n$$

$$= \frac{\$_1}{(1+i)^1} + \frac{\$_2}{(1+i)^2} + \ldots\ldots\ldots\ldots + \frac{\$_n}{(1+i)^n} \qquad \textbf{(2C)}$$

> **Challenge Question**
>
> **G.** Firm ABC is expected to distribute cash dividends of \$2 in year 1, \$1 in year 2, and \$3 in year 3. In year 3, its share is expected to have \$45 market value. What is the fair value of a share of ABC today assuming a 15% interest rate?

2.3: Complications

Recall that, in practice, most banking accounts compound monthly. Hence, to find the PV of an investment with more frequent compounding intervals, Equation (2C) will need to be modified. Because discounting is essentially de-interest, it is necessary to incorporate various compounding intervals in Equation (2C). In general:

$$PV_{m\times n} = \frac{FV}{\left(1+\frac{i}{m}\right)^{m\times n}}$$

$$= FV \times PVIF_{i/m}^{m\times n} \qquad \textbf{(2D)}$$

where

i = annual interest (discount) rate
n = number of years
m = number of times per year that interest is compounded

> **Challenge Question**
>
> **H.** Mark is considering remodeling his house. A 3-year plan is listed as follows.

Year	Item	Spending
1	Kitchen countertop	\$2,500
2	Master bath	\$2,000
3	Study room bookshelf	\$ 800

> He plans to meet the spending by making a lump sum deposit in an account with 12% annual interest rate but compounds monthly. How much should Mark deposit today?

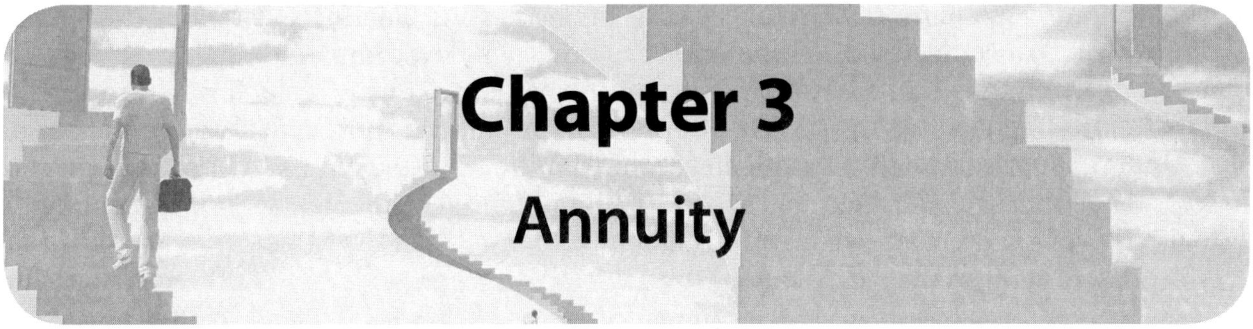

Chapter 3
Annuity

A more frequently encountered situation is where multiple cash flows are of the same amount. Consider, for instance, a very common home mortgage that calls for the borrower to repay the loan by making a series of equal payments for some length of time. In fact, nearly all car loans and home mortgages feature equal payments in every payment interval, usually per month. Such a series of constant cash flows is generally defined as an **annuity**. Based on the timing of the expected cash flows, annuity can be grouped into two categories. One is **ordinary annuity**, defined as a series constant cash flow that occurs at the **end** of each period for some fixed number of periods. The second is **annuity due**, which is an annuity for which the constant cash flows occur at the **beginning** of each period for some fixed number of periods.

3.1: Ordinary Annuity

As defined, an *ordinary annuity* is a series of constant cash flow that occurs at the end of each period. A timeline of ordinary annuity is shown in Figure 3.1.

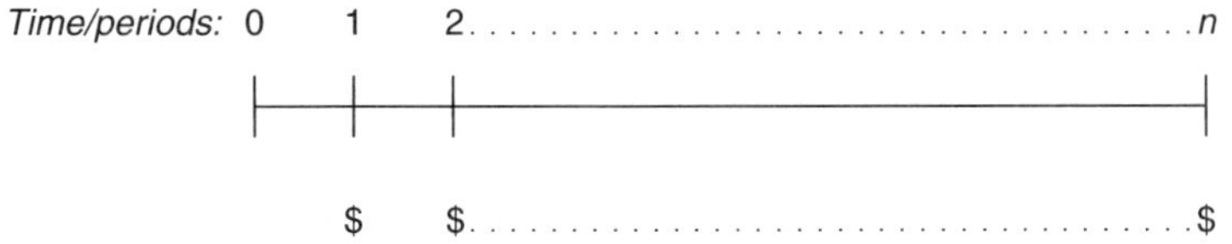

Figure 3.1 Ordinary annuity

We drop the subscript of each cash flow because they are of equal amounts. As usual, Time 0 is today. Time n ($n = 1, 2, \ldots\ldots n$) is considered as the end of each period. In parallel to the definition of ordinary annuity, each cash flow ($) is placed at the end of each period. Note that no cash flow is placed at Time 0 because it is considered as the beginning of period 1. The fact that the series of cash flow is of equal amounts largely simplifies the calculation of its FV and PV. Let's start from the future value of an annuity (FVA) (Figure 3.2).

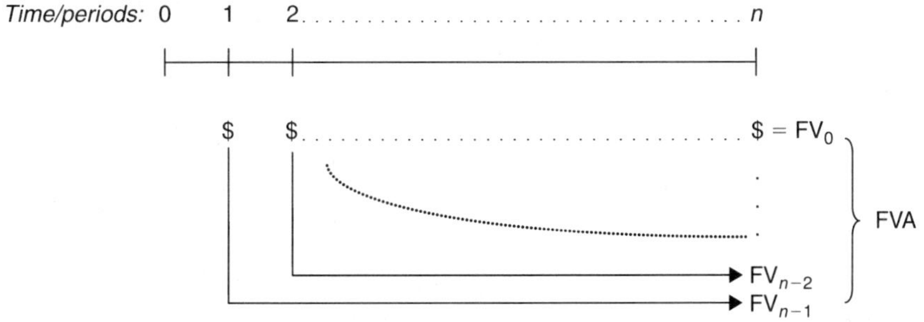

Figure 3.2 Future value of an annuity (FVA)

We compute FVA in much the same way as in Section 1.2. One complication is the length of time a cash flow compounds. For instance, the first cash flow compounds only $n-1$ periods, which is precisely the length of time it stays in the account. The last cash flow occurs at the end of the nth period when the FVA is interested; hence, it does not have time to compound. The FV of this particular cash flow is merely itself. We calculate FVA as follows.

The Future Value of an Annuity (FVA)

$$\begin{aligned} &= FV_0 + FV_1 + FV_2 + \ldots\ldots\ldots + FV_{n-1} \\ &= \$ \times (1+i)^0 + \$ \times (1+i)^1 + \ldots\ldots\ldots + \$ \times (1+i)^{n-1} \\ &= \$ \times \{(1+i)^0 + (1+i)^1 + \ldots\ldots\ldots + (1+i)^{n-1}\} \\ &= \$ \times FVIFA_i^n \end{aligned} \tag{3A}$$

The subscript of each FV in Equation (3A) indicates the number of periods the corresponding cash flow compounds. The calculation of the FVA is largely simplified by using the future value interest factor of annuity ($FVIFA_i^n$) due to the equality of cash flows. The $FVIFA_i^n$ can be found in Appendix D.

Now we turn to the PVA, which is shown in Figure 3.3.

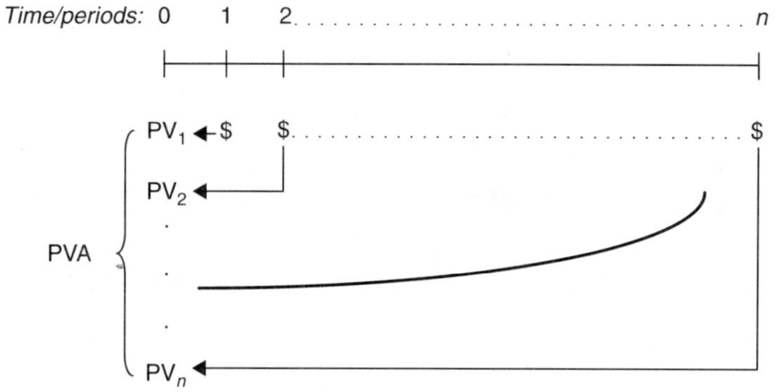

Figure 3.3 Present value of an annuity (PVA)

We compute PVA at Time 0 and in much the same way as in Section 2.2. As in the context of FVA, one complication is the length of time a cash flow discounts. For instance, the last cash flow discounts over the entire n periods because it appears at the very end. We calculate PVA as follows.

The Present Value of an Annuity (PVA)

$$\begin{aligned} &= PV_1 + PV_2 + \ldots\ldots\ldots + PV_n \\ &= \frac{\$}{(1+i)^1} + \frac{\$}{(1+i)^2} + \ldots\ldots\ldots + \frac{\$}{(1+i)^n} \\ &= \$ \times \left\{\frac{1}{(1+i)^1} + \frac{1}{(1+i)^2} + \ldots\ldots\ldots + \frac{1}{(1+i)^n}\right\} \\ &= \$ \times PVIFA_i^n \end{aligned} \tag{3B}$$

The subscript of each PV indicates the length of time it discounts. The $PVIFA_i^n$ is the present value interest factor of annuity, which can be found in Appendix E $PVIFA_i^n$ is used to simplified the calculation due to the equality of each cash flow.

Challenge Question

I. Bill is making a deposit of $2,000 at the end of each year in an account with 5% interest rate. Assume the account compounds annually. How much would he have in the account over 10 years?

3.2: Annuity Due

Annuity due, as defined, is an annuity for which the constant cash flows occur at the **beginning** of each period for some fixed number of periods. A timeline of an annuity due is shown in Figure 3.4.

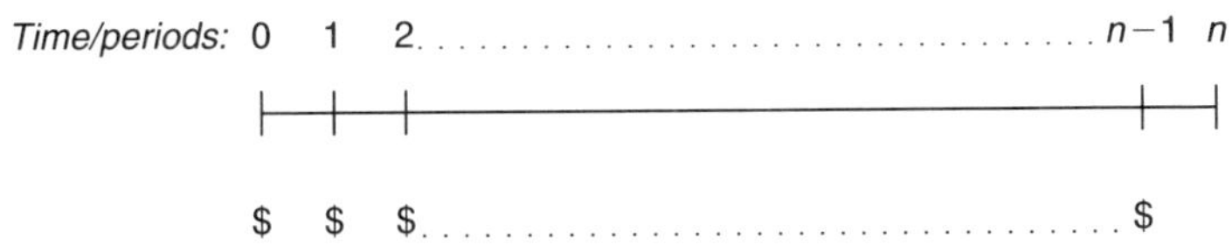

Figure 3.4 Annuity due

Note that an annuity due differs from an ordinary annuity in the timing of the cash flows. Such a difference slightly complicates the calculations of its FV and PV. To make the computations comparable to those of an ordinary annuity, we assume an n-period horizon. Again, Time *0* is today, which is the beginning of the first period. Although Time n (n = 1, 2,....., n) is considered as the end of the nth period in the context of an ordinary annuity, it can also be technically thought of as the beginning of the following period. For instance, December 31, 2008, is the end of 2008. However, considering it as the beginning of 2009 will not seriously impact the calculations of FV or PV. In fact, the effect is minimal. Notice that no cash flow is placed in Time n since it is the beginning of the Time $n+1$. Hence, the cash flows are located at each time period as the ordinary annuity except the cash flows in Time 0 and n.

To maintain the comparability with the future of an ordinary annuity, we compute the FV of an annuity due at Time n as shown in Figure 3.5.

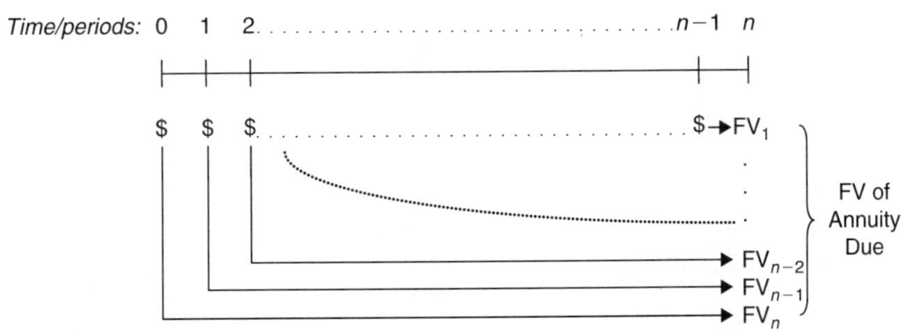

Figure 3.5 Future value of an annuity due

The Future Value of an Annuity Due

$$= FV_1 + FV_2 + \dots\dots\dots + FV_n$$
$$= \$ \times (1 + i)^1 + \dots\dots\dots + \$ \times (1 + i)^n \qquad \textbf{(3C)}$$

Because the first cash flow appears at the very beginning, it compounds over the entire horizon. The subscript of each FV indicates the number of periods the corresponding cash flow compounds. Unfortunately, there is no specific interest factor designed to simplify the calculation as in the context of an ordinary annuity. However, because the two types of annuities are fairly similar, we can take advantage of the ordinary annuity interest factors with a minor modification in the equations. We will come back to this with an example in the end of this section. Now let's turn to the PV of an annuity due (Figure 3.6).

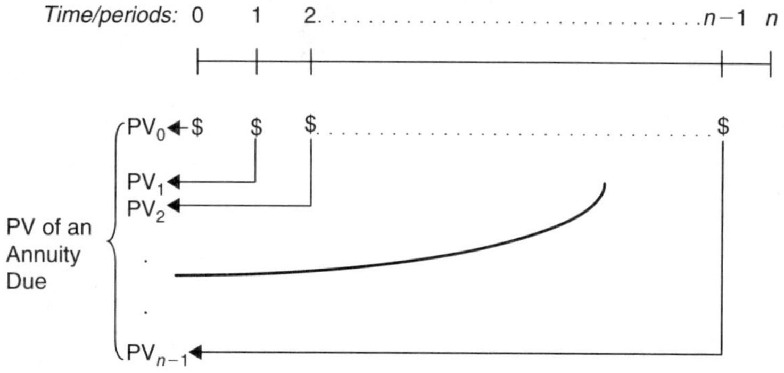

Figure 3.6 Present value of an annuity due

The Present Value of an Annuity Due

$$= PV_0 + PV_1 + PV_2 + \dots\dots\dots + PV_{n-1}$$
$$= \frac{\$}{(1 + i)^0} + \frac{\$}{(1 + i)^1} + \frac{\$}{(1 + i)^2} + \dots\dots\dots + \frac{\$}{(1 + i)^{n-1}} \qquad \textbf{(3D)}$$

The subscript of each PV suggests the length of time the cash flow discounts. We are calculating the PV of the annuity due at Time 0. Therefore, the first cash flow does not discount since it appears at Time 0. The last cash flow only discounts $n - 1$ periods.

Unfortunately, as noted, there is no interest factor specifically designed for an annuity due. However, Equations (3C) and (3D) are fairly similar to (3A) and (3B). This comes with no surprise because there is merely one cash flow difference in ordinary annuity and annuity due. We attempt simplifying the computations of the FV and PV of an annuity due with an example. Suppose an annuity due has four cash flows of $500 each. The relevant interest/discount rate is 8%. The timeline of the annuity due is shown in the first line of Figure 3.7.

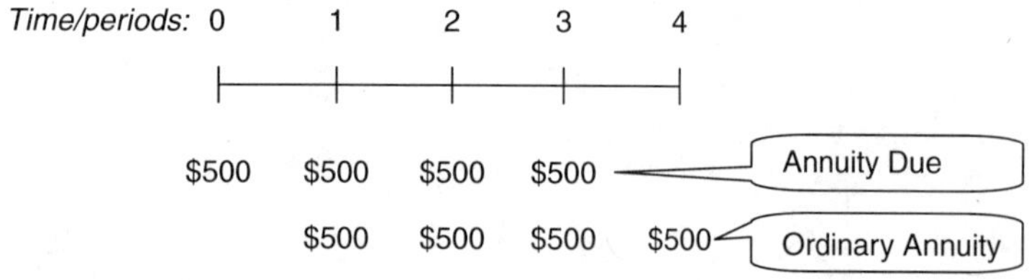

Figure 3.7 Annuity due of $500 over 4 years

Notice how the cash flows of the annuity due are similar with those for a 4-year ordinary annuity (second line in Figure 3.7). The difference is merely the timing of the cash flows. Now let's try the FV of the annuity due and ordinary annuity and show how they are related. Needless to say, we are computing the FV at the end of year 4.

Following Equation (3C),

The Future Value of an Annuity Due

$$= FV_1 + FV_2 + FV_3 + FV_4$$
$$= 500 \times (1 + 8\%)^1 + 500 \times (1 + 8\%)^2 + 500 \times (1 + 8\%)^3 + 500 \times (1 + 8\%)^4$$
$$= 2{,}433.30$$

Now, we calculate the FV of the comparable ordinary annuity by Equation (3A),

The Future Value of an Annuity (FVA)

$$= FV_0 + FV_1 + FV_2 + FV_3$$
$$= 500 \times (1 + 8\%)^0 + 500 \times (1 + 8\%)^1 + 500 \times (1 + 8\%)^2 + 500 \times (1 + 8\%)^3$$
$$= 500 \times \left\{(1 + 8\%)^0 + (1 + 8\%)^1 + (1 + 8\%)^2 + (1 + 8\%)^3\right\}$$
$$= 500 \times FVIFA^4_{8\%}$$
$$= 2{,}253.05$$

Hence, in the current example, the FV of the annuity due is \$2,433.30 while the FV of the ordinary annuity is \$2,253.05. One thing to note is that, in the context of FV, because the cash flows of an annuity due occur in the beginning of each period instead of the end, we practically compound every cash flow by one period more than it is with ordinary annuity. This is particularly true while comparing the two calculations above. Following this line, the FVs of the two types of annuity can be related as follows:

$$\textit{Future Value of an Annuity Due} = \textit{Future Value of an Ordinary Annuity} \times (1 + i) \qquad \textbf{(3E)}$$

For practice in the current example, verify that if we multiply the FV of the ordinary annuity by (1 + 8%), we get \$2,433.30, which is exactly the FV of this annuity due.

Now, let's verify whether this relationship also holds for the PV. Following Equation (3D), we compute the PV of the annuity due.

The Present Value of an Annuity Due

$$= PV_0 + PV_1 + PV_2 + PV_3$$
$$= \frac{500}{(1 + 8\%)^0} + \frac{500}{(1 + 8\%)^1} + \frac{500}{(1 + 8\%)^2} + \frac{500}{(1 + 8\%)^3}$$
$$= 1{,}788.55$$

We calculate the PV of the ordinary annuity by Equation (3B).

The Present Value of an Annuity (PVA)

$$= PV_1 + PV_2 + PV_3 + PV_4$$

$$= \frac{500}{(1+8\%)^1} + \frac{500}{(1+8\%)^2} + \frac{500}{(1+8\%)^3} + \frac{500}{(1+8\%)^4}$$

$$= 500 \times \left\{ \frac{1}{(1+8\%)^1} + \frac{1}{(1+8\%)^2} + \frac{1}{(1+8\%)^3} + \frac{1}{(1+8\%)^4} \right\}$$

$$= 500 \times PVIFA_{8\%}^{4}$$

$$= 1{,}656.05$$

Again, we find that multiplying the PV of the ordinary annuity (PVA) by (1 + 8%), we get $1,788.53, which is fairly close to the FV of the annuity due. Therefore, the relationship still holds.

$$\textit{Present Value of an Annuity Due} = \textit{Present Value of an Ordinary Annuity} \times (1 + i) \qquad \textbf{(3F)}$$

In the context of PV, because the cash flows of an annuity due occur in the beginning of each period instead of the end, we essentially discount every cash flow by one period less than it is with ordinary annuity. Hence, one way to fix this is simply multiplying the PV of the ordinary annuity by $(1 + i)$, which gives us Equation (3F).

In sum, Equations (3E) and (3F) suggest a much easier way to calculate the future or PV of an annuity due. The FV and PV of an annuity due can be found by multiplying the comparable ordinary annuity value by (1+interest rate). In other words, we can now use the interest factors for ordinary annuity in the calculation of annuity due values.

$$\textit{Annuity Due Value} = \textit{Ordinary Annuity Value} \times (1 + i) \qquad \textbf{(3G)}$$

Challenge Questions

J. You are setting up a trust fund for your daughter today. The fund is to pay $30,000 every year for the next 20 years. The money in the trust fund earns 10% compounded annually. How much money must be put in the fund today to ensure the next 20 years of payments?

K. Paul plans to retire in 15 years. He would like to spend $50,000 a year in his retirement years. Paul expects to live for 20 years after retiring. His retirement account can earn 8% a year. How much money does Paul need in his retirement account when he retires to be able to live the lifestyle he desires?

L. Suppose you win a $1 million lottery. However, you will not be paid immediately with the prize but gradually. The government provides you with the payment schedule. In short, you will be paid $50,000 a year for the following 20 years but the first payment is made today. What is the value of the lottery today assuming a 10% interest rate?

3.3: Perpetuities

Perpetuity is a special type of an annuity in which the series of constant cash flows continue *forever*. The timeline is shown in Figure 3.8.

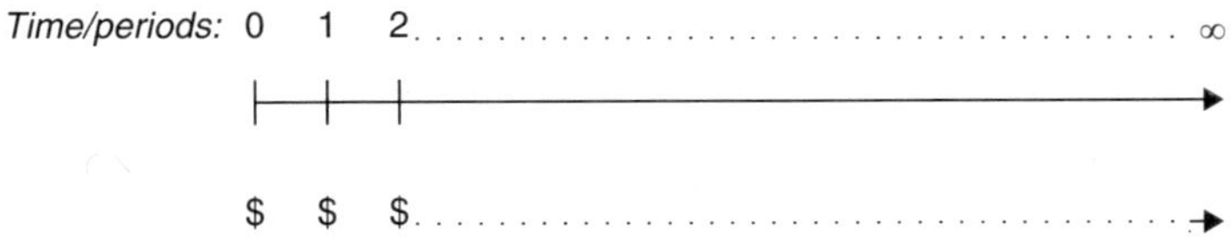

Figure 3.8 Timeline of a perpetuity

Because the stream of cash flows is perpetual, we obviously cannot calculate its PV by discounting each one. Fortunately, valuing a perpetuity gives us an important property, making the calculation of the PV a very simple case:

$$\textit{Present Value of an Perpetuity} = \frac{\$}{i} \qquad \textbf{(3H)}$$

where

$\$$ = the cash flow each period
i = interest rate per period

Challenge Questions

Assume an investment offers a perpetual cash flow of $800 every year. Further assume a 5% interest rate.

M. What is the present value of such investment?

N. What is the future value of the investment?

Chapter 4
Applications of Future and Present Values

In this chapter, we learn how to apply the concepts of FV and PV in some real world situations. In fact, we apply them more often than we imagine. This chapter is structured by various examples. Note that the application of the concepts is not limited to these examples.

4.1: CD Account

The time certificate of deposits (CD) is a straightforward application of FV. Consider, for instance, Tom opens a 15-month term CD account with \$2,000. Assume, for simplicity, the interest rate is 12%. How much would Tom have at the end of the term? There are two things worth a note. First, CD accounts compound monthly. Second, regardless of the term of the account, the interest rate is always quoted annually. A timeline of the current example is shown in Figure 4.1.

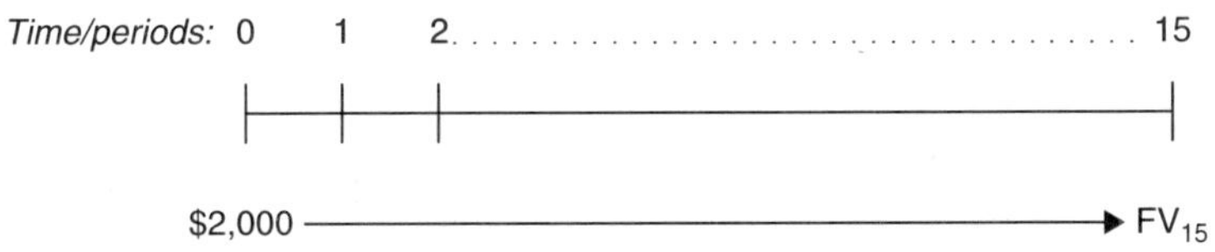

Figure 4.1 Timeline of a 15-month CD account

Following Equation (1D), clearly, we have

$$
\begin{aligned}
FV_{15} &= 2{,}000 \times \left(1 + \frac{12\%}{12}\right)^{15} \\
&= 2{,}000 \times FVIF_{1\%}^{15} \\
&= 2{,}322
\end{aligned}
$$

Recall that with monthly compounding, the actual return by investing in the CD account, Tom expects to earn more than the quoted annual interest rate (i.e., 12%). The rate of return that captures this concept is the effective annual rate (EAR). Because the EAR is calculated on an annual basis, we need to find the FV in 1 year, not in 15 months, regardless of the fact that it is a 15-month term CD.

$$FV_{12} = 2{,}000 \times \left(1 + \frac{12\%}{12}\right)^{12}$$
$$= 2{,}000 \times FVIF_{1\%}^{12}$$
$$= 2{,}253.6$$
$$EAR = \frac{2253.6 - 2{,}000}{2{,}000} \times 100\%$$
$$= 12.68\%$$

The EAR is clearly higher than the quoted interest rate due to the monthly compounding interval.

4.2: College Fund

In this example, let us assume that Mary is setting up a college fund for her son, Kevin. Suppose Kevin is currently a high school senior and expects to go to college 1 year from now. On average, a college costs $20,000 a year including tuition, fees, and living expenses. He expects to stay in college for 4 years. How much should Mary deposit/invest in an account with 12% interest rate today to meet the college expenses? Further assume that the account compounds annually.

Needless to say, the 4-year college expense is a type of annuity because it involves constant annual cash flows. Let's look at the timeline first (Figure 4.2).

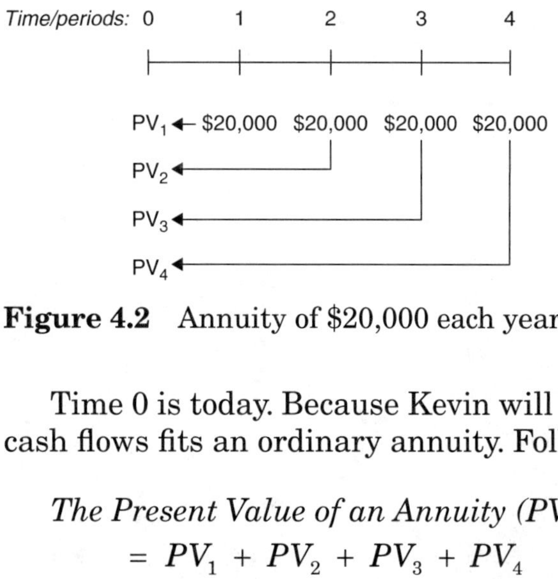

Figure 4.2 Annuity of $20,000 each year for 4 years

Time 0 is today. Because Kevin will be going to college 1 year from now, the series of cash flows fits an ordinary annuity. Following Equation (3B),

The Present Value of an Annuity (PVA)

$$= PV_1 + PV_2 + PV_3 + PV_4$$
$$= \frac{20{,}000}{(1+12\%)^1} + \frac{20{,}000}{(1+12\%)^2} + \frac{20{,}000}{(1+12\%)^3} + \frac{20{,}000}{(1+12\%)^4}$$
$$= 20{,}000 \times \left\{\frac{1}{(1+12\%)^1} + \frac{1}{(1+12\%)^2} + \frac{1}{(1+12\%)^3} + \frac{1}{(1+12\%)^4}\right\}$$
$$= 20{,}000 \times PVIFA_{12\%}^{4}$$
$$= 60{,}746$$

Hence, Mary will need to deposit $60,746 in this account and, most important, let it roll over for 4 years. At the end of 4 years, the time Kevin graduates from college, the remaining funds in the account will be fully exhausted.

Now, let's remove one of the assumptions to make the example more realistic. Recall that most banking accounts are compounded monthly instead of yearly. With monthly compounding, the amount of money Mary would have to deposit should be less than what we just calculated.

The Present Value of an Annuity (PVA)

$$= PV_1 + PV_2 + PV_3 + PV_4$$
$$= \frac{20{,}000}{\left(1 + \frac{12\%}{12}\right)^{12}} + \frac{20{,}000}{\left(1 + \frac{12\%}{12}\right)^{24}} + \frac{20{,}000}{\left(1 + \frac{12\%}{12}\right)^{36}} + \frac{20{,}000}{\left(1 + \frac{12\%}{12}\right)^{48}}$$
$$= 20{,}000 \times \left\{\frac{1}{(1 + 1\%)^{12}} + \frac{1}{(1 + 1\%)^{24}} + \frac{1}{(1 + 1\%)^{36}} + \frac{1}{(1 + 1\%)^{48}}\right\}$$
$$= 20{,}000 \times 2.9942$$
$$= 59{,}884$$

As expected, with monthly compounding, Mary only needs to deposit $59,884 to meet the goal.

Now, let's extend the timeline to represent the example as a long-term plan. Assume Kevin is now only 5 years old and expects to go to college at age 18. Mary is setting up the college fund for him now. The college expenses and interest rate remain the same. For simplicity, assume the account compounds yearly. Clearly, Mary has two options. Option 1 calls for a lump sum deposit/investment to be made in the account and to let it roll over until Kevin's graduation from college. Option 2 suggests a much easier way, at least financially—a yearly deposit over 13 years. In other words, Mary deposits a certain amount of money yearly until Kevin goes to college.

Option 1: Lump Sum Investment

Because Kevin is 5 years old, it will be 13 years until he goes to college. In Figure 4.3, the timeline starts from when Kevin is 5, which is Time 0 in our terminology.

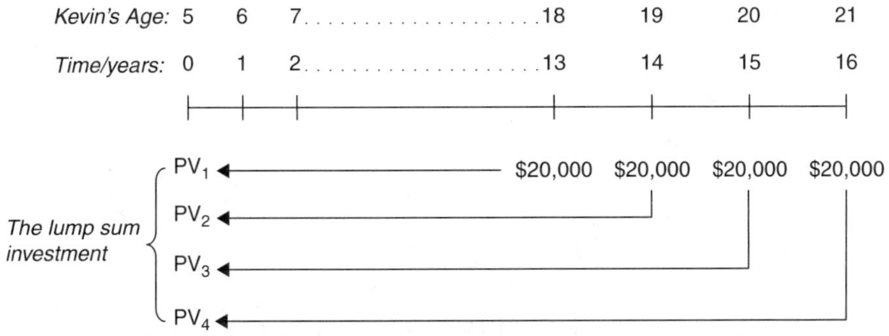

Figure 4.3 Lump sum investment

The lump sum investment is practically the original example except for the much longer time period (13 years) until Kevin goes to college.

$$
\begin{aligned}
&\textit{The Lump Sum Investment}\\
&= PV_1 + PV_2 + PV_3 + PV_4\\
&= \frac{20,000}{(1+12\%)^{13}} + \frac{20,000}{(1+12\%)^{14}} + \frac{20,000}{(1+12\%)^{15}} + \frac{20,000}{(1+12\%)^{16}}\\
&= 20,000 \times \left\{\frac{1}{(1+12\%)^{13}} + \frac{1}{(1+12\%)^{14}} + \frac{1}{(1+12\%)^{15}} + \frac{1}{(1+12\%)^{16}}\right\}\\
&= 15,592.24
\end{aligned}
$$

Hence, Mary will deposit $15,592.24 in the account today. Notice that the amount is much less than previous examples because there is more time.

Option 2: Yearly Investment

Option 2 is computationally more complex than Option 1. However, it is more financially feasible. There are two steps involved. First, we need to find how much money is needed to meet the 4-year college expenses at the time Kevin goes to college. Second, once the amount is determined, a yearly deposit can be determined. Figure 4.4 shows the timeline.

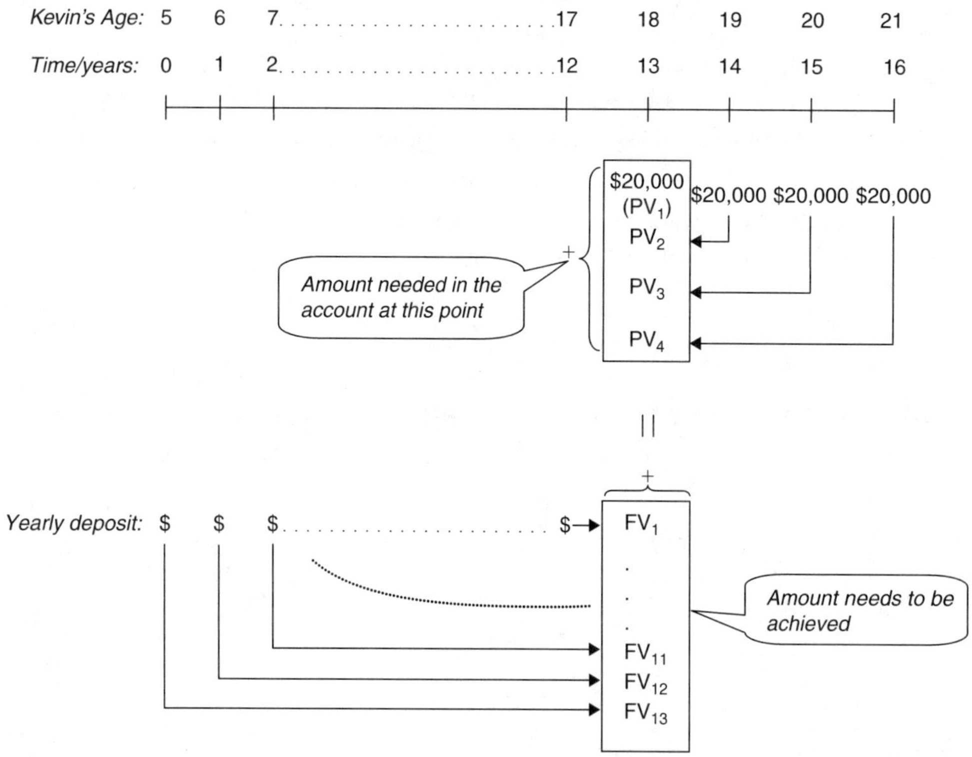

Figure 4.4 Yearly investment

Hence, first we need to find the amount of money that is needed in the account when Kevin turns 18 years old. Because he will need $20,000 a year for 4 years, we discount the series of college expenses as shown in Figure 4.4. Note the timing of the college expenses suggests an annuity due.

Following Equation (3D), we have

The amount needed in the account while kevin goes to college

$$= PV_0 + PV_1 + PV_2 + PV_3$$
$$= \frac{20,000}{(1 + 12\%)^0} + \frac{20,000}{(1 + 12\%)^1} + \frac{20,000}{(1 + 12\%)^2} + \frac{20,000}{(1 + 12\%)^3}$$
$$= 68,036.62$$

> Note that there is a much easier way. We can take advantage on the ordinary annuity Equation.
>
> Following Equation (3G),
>
> The amount needed in the account while Kevin goes to college
> $= \text{Ordinary Annuity Value} \times (1 + i)$
> $= 20,000 \times PVIFA^4_{12\%} \times (1 + 12\%)$
> $= 68035.52$

Now we have the amount of money needed to meet the college expenses. Next we figure out how to arrive at such an amount via yearly investment in the account. Assume \$ is the yearly deposit. Starting from today when Kevin is 5 years old (Time 0), Mary has 13 years until Kevin is 18 years old to arrive at the required amount. The timing of the constant yearly investment calls for an annuity due. Following Equation (3C),

$$68,036.62 = \$ \times (1 + 12\%)^{13} + \$ \times (1 + 12\%)^{12} + \ldots\ldots\ldots + \$ \times (1 + 12\%)^1$$
$$= \$ \times \{(1 + 12\%)^{13} + (1 + 12\%)^{12} + \ldots\ldots\ldots (1 + 12\%)^1\}$$

Note that we can obtain an easier solution by using equation (3G). Hence, the above equation becomes

$$= \text{ordinary annuity value} \times (1 + 12\%)$$
$$= \$ \times FVIFA^{13}_{12\%} \times (1 + 12\%)$$

Now, solve for \$

$$\$ = \frac{68,036.62}{FVIFA^{13}_{12\%} \times (1 + 12\%)}$$
$$= 2,167.29$$

Hence, Mary will need to invest \$2167.29 in the college fund annually starting now to arrive at \$68,036.62 in 13 years.

Challenge Question

O. Now use the same example but assume the account compounds monthly. Redo Options 1 and 2.

4.3: Retirement Plan

Consider the *challenge question (F)* in Section 2.1 for a moment. Clearly, Sue has two options of arriving at $500,000 in 15 years at retirement. One is a lump sum deposit today (as the question asked). The other, which is more financially realistic, is making a deposit periodically (e.g., yearly) over 15 years. Both options could help her attain her goal. However, the second one is easier, at least financially, because it involves with a much smaller yearly investment than one lump sum investment. How much is the annual investment?

Let's look at the timeline first (Figure 4.5).

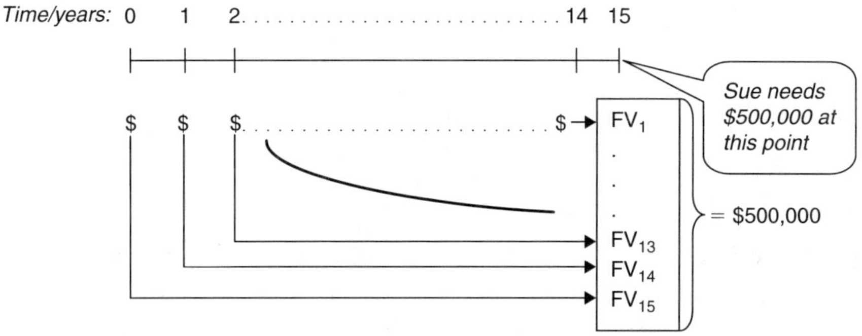

Figure 4.5 Yearly investment in a retirement account

We place $500,000 at year 15 because it is the point at which Sue is planning to retire. The yearly investment in the account is the $s starting from today. Hence, the series of cash flow implies an annuity due. We are solving for the $s.

$$\begin{aligned} 500{,}000 &= \$ \times (1 + 6\%)^{15} + \$ \times (1 + 6\%)^{14} + \ldots\ldots + \$ \times (1 + 6\%)^{1} \\ &= \$ \times \{(1 + 6\%)^{15} + (1 + 6\%)^{14} + \ldots\ldots + (1 + 6\%)^{1}\} \end{aligned}$$

Again, following Equation (3G). The above equation becomes

$$\begin{aligned} &= \text{ordinary annuity value} \times (1 + 6\%) \\ &= \$ \times FVIFA^{15}_{6\%} \times (1 + 6\%) \end{aligned}$$

Now, solve for $

$$\begin{aligned} \$ &= \frac{500{,}000}{FVIFA^{15}_{6\%} \times (1 + 6\%)} \\ &= 20{,}265.43 \end{aligned}$$

4.4: Car Financing

Assume Tom is buying a car with a \$5,000 down payment. The final price is \$30,000. Tom plans to finance the rest of the price over 3 years. The APR (annual percentage rate) is 12%. Assuming there are no other fees, how much is the monthly car payment?

The APR is merely the annual interest rate, yet car payments are made monthly. Hence, a car loan compounds monthly. Tom is actually borrowing \$25,000 after the \$5,000 down payment. Note that the \$25,000 is borrowed today and, hence, it is placed at Time 0. The first payment is made a month later and all payments are of an equal amount. Therefore, the payment stream is in fact an ordinary annuity (Figure 4.6).

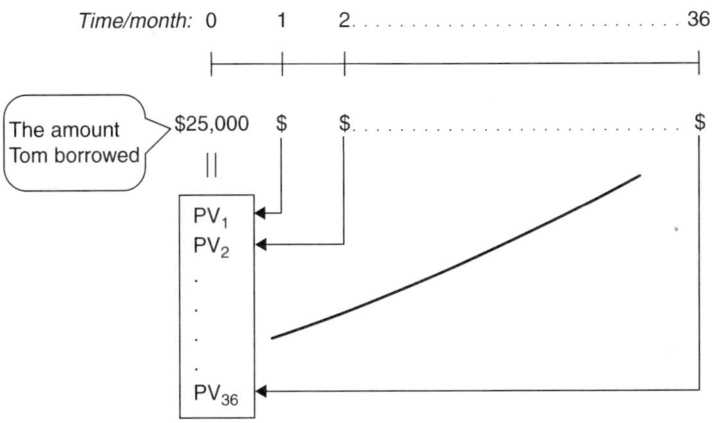

Figure 4.6 Car payment

$$
\begin{aligned}
25{,}000 &= PV_1 + PV_2 + \dots\dots\dots + PV_{36} \\
&= \frac{\$}{\left(1+\frac{12\%}{12}\right)^1} + \frac{\$}{\left(1+\frac{12\%}{12}\right)^2} + \dots\dots\dots + \frac{\$}{\left(1+\frac{12\%}{12}\right)^{36}} \\
&= \$ \times PVIFA_{1\%}^{36}
\end{aligned}
$$

Solve for \$,

$$
\begin{aligned}
\$ &= \frac{25{,}000}{PVIFA_{1\%}^{36}} \\
&= 830.36
\end{aligned}
$$

One variation of the example is working reversely to determine the affordable price of a car. Suppose Jack has a monthly income of \$3,500. After taxes and living expenses, he is able to set aside \$350 a month for a car loan. He is planning to finance a car within this budget for 5 years and he is able to put \$6,000 down. What is the right price for him? Assume 12% APR.

The \$350 a month for 5 years is merely the payment stream. With this in mind, we are simply determining how much Jack can afford to borrow with such a series of repayment (Figure 4.7).

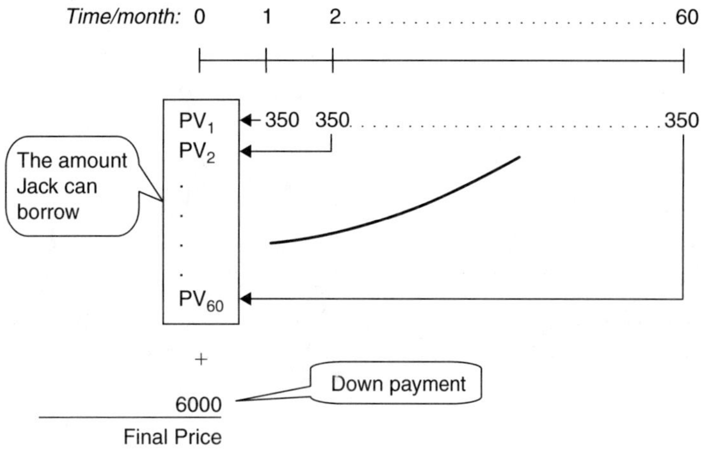

Figure 4.7 Affordable car price

The amount Jack can borrow

$$
\begin{aligned}
&= PV_1 + PV_2 + \dots\dots\dots + PV_{60} \\
&= \frac{350}{\left(1+\frac{12\%}{12}\right)^1} + \frac{350}{\left(1+\frac{12\%}{12}\right)^2} + \dots\dots\dots + \frac{350}{\left(1+\frac{12\%}{12}\right)^{60}} \\
&= 350 \times PVIFA_{1\%}^{60} \\
&= 15{,}734.26
\end{aligned}
$$

The price that Jack an afford (the final price)

$$
\begin{aligned}
&= 15734.26 + 6{,}000 \\
&= 21{,}734.26
\end{aligned}
$$

Therefore, with the budget of a \$350 monthly payment with \$6,000 down, Jack can afford a car with a price tag of \$21,734.26.

4.5: Mortgage

The final application of the FV and PV concepts is a house mortgage. A mortgage is very similar to a car loan in that it also involves monthly payments except the time horizon is much longer. Let's assume Claudia is planning to buy a home with a price tag at \$200,000. She is able to put 20% down—that is, \$40,000. According to her credit history, she is able to obtain a 25-year fixed-rate mortgage at a 6% rate. What is the monthly payment? For simplicity, assume no fees.

Again, because the first payment is usually made 1 month later, the mortgage payment stream implies an ordinary annuity (Figure 4.8).

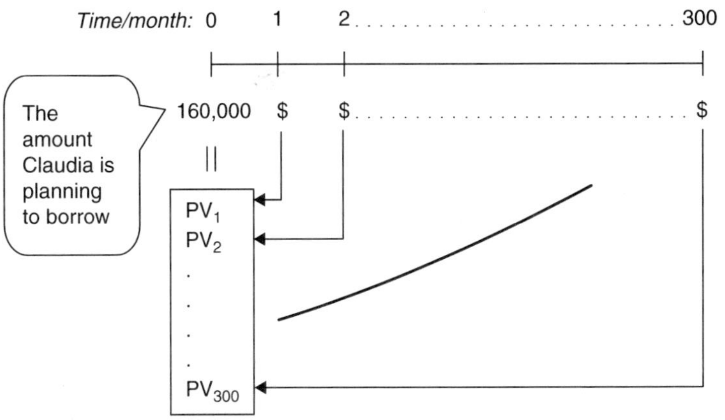

Figure 4.8 House mortgage monthly payment

$$
\begin{aligned}
160{,}000 &= PV_1 + PV_2 + \dots\dots\dots + PV_{300} \\
&= \frac{\$}{\left(1+\frac{6\%}{12}\right)^1} + \frac{\$}{\left(1+\frac{6\%}{12}\right)^2} + \dots\dots\dots + \frac{\$}{\left(1+\frac{6\%}{12}\right)^{300}} \\
&= \$ \times PVIFA_{0.5\%}^{300}
\end{aligned}
$$

Solve for \$,

$$
\begin{aligned}
\$ &= \frac{160{,}000}{PVIFA_{0.5\%}^{300}} \\
&= 1{,}030.88
\end{aligned}
$$

Hence, if Claudia bought the house, her monthly mortgage payment would be \$1,030.88 for 25 years.

One practical variation is to find an affordable housing price. Say, Thomas is considering buying a house. After living expenses, he is able to set aside \$1,200 a month. With his credit history, he is confident that he can acquire a 30-year fixed rate mortgage at 6%. Further assume he can put \$20,000 down. What is the reasonable house price for him?

Clearly, the mortgage payment stream is \$1,200 a month for 30 years. Hence, the amount Thomas could borrow is merely the PV of the serises of payments. Consequently, the reasonable price is merely the summation of the amount he could borrow and the down payment (Figure 4.9).

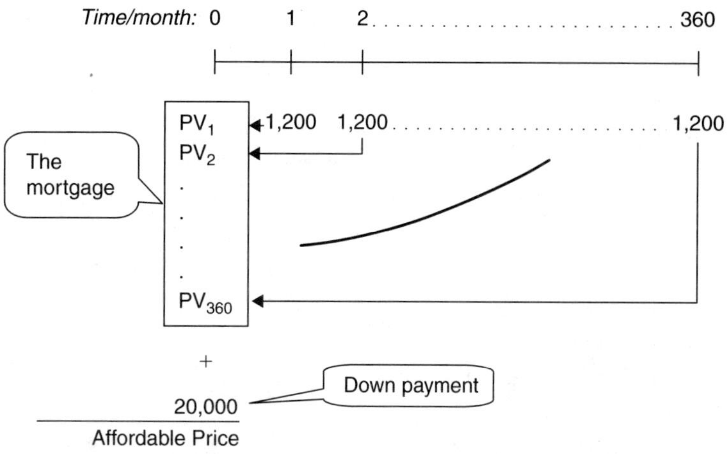

Figure 4.9 Affordable house price

The amount Thomas can borrow (the mortgage)

$$= PV_1 + PV_2 + \dots\dots\dots + PV_{360}$$

$$= \frac{1,200}{\left(1+\frac{6\%}{12}\right)^1} + \frac{1,200}{\left(1+\frac{6\%}{12}\right)^2} + \dots\dots\dots + \frac{1,200}{\left(1+\frac{6\%}{12}\right)^{360}}$$

$$= 1,200 \times PVIFA_{0.5\%}^{360}$$

$$= 200,149.94$$

The price that Thomas an afford (the affordable price)

$$= \$200,149.94 + \$20,000$$

$$= \$220,149.94$$

Chapter 5
Conclusion

The idea that money has a time value is one of the most fundamental but critical concepts in the field of finance. The concept indicates that a dollar today is worth more than a dollar received in the future because a dollar today can be invested in somewhere and earns interest. Thus, money grows over time.

This book has introduced you to the basic ideas of the time value of money and various applications of the concepts. We first cover the very simple cases—the FV and PV with only one cash flow over one and multiple periods. We show the concepts and procedures of compounding and discounting and how interest rate relates to the procedures. Due to compounding, money grows disproportionally. Most important, we observe that time plays a crucial role. To arrive at a targeted amount of money at certain point in the future, the more time we have, the less present investment we need to commit.

Second, we extend our discussion in the context of multiple cash flows and periods. We further the concept by allowing multiple investments (i.e., cash flows), which is much more common in reality. Consider, for example, the periodic investment in mutual funds. One major advantage of allowing multiple cash flows is that it makes various financial planning a lot easier than making only one lump sum investment. This concept has tremendous applications, including (but not limited to) college funds, car financing, and mortgages as we round up the discussion. The computation of the FV and PV of multiple cash flows hinges on the interest rate (or discount rate), which is impacted directly by a number of external factors, such as the money market and monetary policy. As a result, the calculations discussed here help you to better understand the effect of various policies, particularly on your economic well-being.

To enhance your understanding of the concepts and sharpen your skills at using FV and PV, the questions in Appendix A provide excellent practice and application.

Appendix A
Practice Questions

1. Your local bank offers you an interest rate of 4% on a 2-year certificate of deposit (CD). If you deposit $1,000 in the 2-year CD,
   a. how much will your deposit be worth in 2 years if the account compounds yearly?
   b. how much will your deposit be worth in 2 years if the account compounds semiannually?
   c. how much will your deposit be worth in 2 years if the account compounds quarterly?
2. Explain clearly how compound interest differs from simple interest.
3. John has $14,000 in cash. He has two choices on investing the money. Choice (a), he can invest in a mutual fund earning 8% annually. Choice (b), he can wait, enjoy some of it, and invest $11,000 in a mutual fund earning 10% annually in 2 years. Further assume John needs to cash in at the end of 10 years from now. Which option will he choose?
4. Suppose Tom is planning to take a vacation to Europe in 2 years. His local bank offers a 2-year certificate of deposit (CD) that pays 6%. How much money does Tom need to set aside today to generate $5,000 when he leaves for Europe?
5. Judy wins a $1 million lottery. Instead of paying her a lump sum of $1 million today, the government offers her a payment stream of $50,000 a year over 20 years. The first payment will be made today. What is the value of the lottery assuming 5% interest rate?
6. You are negotiating a 3-month contract with an employer. He offers you two alternatives of wage payments. You can receive $2,000 per month or $1,000 every 2 weeks.
   a. If the discount rate is 12%, which alternative should you choose?
   b. If the discount rate is 6%, which alternative should you choose?
7. Mike is 35 years old and he is planning to retire in 25 years. He expects to live 20 more years when he retires. He figures he would need $50,000 a year to live his life style after retirement.
   a. How much money will Mike need at retirement assume 6% interest rate?
   b. Assume Mike is planning a lump sum investment today with 6% interest rate to arrive at the figure in (a). How much is the lump sum?
   c. Instead of a lump sum investment, Mike is planning a yearly investment. Still assume 6% interest rate, how much is the yearly investment in order to arrive at the amount in (a)?
   d. Now, assume the interest rate is 2%, re-do (b) and (c). Compare to (b) and (c), what do you find?

8. A local bank offers 12% on a 15-month certificate of deposit (CD).
   a. Assume investing $1,000 in this CD account, how much will we have while it matures?
   b. What is the Effective Annual Rate (EAR) of this CD?
9. David borrows $2,000 at 12% from a bank and hopes to pay it off monthly over 18 month.
   a. What is the monthly payment?
   b. What is the Effective Annual Rate (EAR) of this loan?
10. Tim is purchasing a car with a price tag of $22,000. He can afford $5,000 down payment. The car dealer offers him 12% Annual Percentage Rate (APR: car loan interest rate) over 3 years. How much is the monthly car payment?
11. Tommy is purchasing a house. He can set aside $1,500 per month for the mortgage payments. He can afford $20,000 down payment. With his credit score, he could get a 25-year fixed rate mortgage at 12%. What is the reasonable house price for him?
12. Assume there is an investment opportunity available. The investment pays $150 yearly forever. What is the value of this investment assuming 4% interest rate?
13. You are setting up a college fund for your son who is going to college in 3 years. The tuition bill is $15,000 a year for four years. Assume the discount rate is 6%.
   a. How much money will you need while your son goes to college?
   b. What is the amount of money you need to put down as a lump sum today to generate the figure in (a)?
   c. Assume you are able to put some income aside every year to generate the amount in (a). How much should it be?
   d. Compare (b) and (c). Conclude your finding.
14. Steven went to college on a student loan of $80,000 at 12%. The loan requires monthly repayment over 5 years upon graduation. Upon his graduation 2 years ago, Steven started to pay it off. Steven is now considering pay it off once and for all. How much should he pay?
15. Brian mortgaged $200,000 on his house 10 years ago. The mortgage was 25-year fixed rate mortgage at 12%. He realizes today that a refinance opportunity available at 6% for the rest of his mortgage's term. Assume there are no additional fees.
   a. What was Brian's monthly mortgage payment?
   b. How much Brian still owe currently?
   c. If Brian took the refinance, what is his new monthly mortgage payment?

Appendix B

Future Value Interest Factor (FVIF)

Compound Sum of $1–$FVIF_{i\%, n \text{ years}}$

n	1%	2%	3%	4%	5%	6%	7%	8%	9%	10%
1	1.010	1.020	1.030	1.040	1.050	1.060	1.070	1.080	1.090	1.100
2	1.020	1.040	1.061	1.082	1.102	1.124	1.145	1.166	1.188	1.210
3	1.030	1.061	1.093	1.125	1.158	1.191	1.225	1.260	1.295	1.331
4	1.041	1.082	1.126	1.170	1.216	1.262	1.311	1.360	1.412	1.464
5	1.051	1.104	1.159	1.217	1.276	1.338	1.403	1.469	1.539	1.611
6	1.062	1.126	1.194	1.265	1.340	1.419	1.501	1.587	1.677	1.772
7	1.072	1.149	1.230	1.316	1.407	1.504	1.606	1.714	1.828	1.949
8	1.083	1.172	1.267	1.369	1.477	1.594	1.718	1.851	1.993	2.144
9	1.094	1.195	1.305	1.423	1.551	1.689	1.838	1.999	2.172	2.358
10	1.105	1.219	1.344	1.480	1.629	1.791	1.967	2.159	2.367	2.594
11	1.116	1.243	1.384	1.539	1.710	1.898	2.105	2.332	2.580	2.853
12	1.127	1.268	1.426	1.601	1.796	2.012	2.252	2.518	2.813	3.138
13	1.138	1.294	1.469	1.665	1.886	2.133	2.410	2.720	3.066	3.452
14	1.149	1.319	1.513	1.732	1.980	2.261	2.579	2.937	3.342	3.797
15	1.161	1.346	1.558	1.801	2.079	2.397	2.759	3.172	3.642	4.177
16	1.173	1.373	1.605	1.873	2.183	2.540	2.952	3.426	3.970	4.595
17	1.184	1.400	1.653	1.948	2.292	2.693	3.159	3.700	4.328	5.054
18	1.196	1.428	1.702	2.026	2.407	2.854	3.380	3.996	4.717	5.560
19	1.208	1.457	1.753	2.107	2.527	3.026	3.616	4.316	5.142	6.116
20	1.220	1.486	1.806	2.191	2.653	3.207	3.870	4.661	5.604	6.727
21	1.232	1.516	1.860	2.279	2.786	3.399	4.140	5.034	6.109	7.400
22	1.245	1.546	1.916	2.370	2.925	3.603	4.430	5.436	6.658	8.140
23	1.257	1.577	1.974	2.465	3.071	3.820	4.740	5.871	7.258	8.954
24	1.270	1.608	2.033	2.563	3.225	4.049	5.072	6.341	7.911	9.850
25	1.282	1.641	2.094	2.666	3.386	4.292	5.427	6.848	8.623	10.834
30	1.348	1.811	2.427	3.243	4.322	5.743	7.612	10.062	13.267	17.449
40	1.489	2.208	3.262	4.801	7.040	10.285	14.974	21.724	31.408	45.258
50	1.645	2.691	4.384	7.106	11.467	18.419	29.456	46.900	74.354	117.386

n	11%	12%	13%	14%	15%	16%	17%	18%	19%	20%
1	1.110	1.120	1.130	1.140	1.150	1.160	1.170	1.180	1.190	1.200
2	1.232	1.254	1.277	1.300	1.322	1.346	1.369	1.392	1.416	1.440
3	1.368	1.405	1.443	1.482	1.521	1.561	1.602	1.643	1.685	1.728
4	1.518	1.574	1.630	1.689	1.749	1.811	1.874	1.939	2.005	2.074
5	1.685	1.762	1.842	1.925	2.011	2.100	2.192	2.288	2.386	2.488
6	1.870	1.974	2.082	2.195	2.313	2.436	2.565	2.700	2.840	2.986
7	2.076	2.211	2.353	2.502	2.660	2.826	3.001	3.185	3.379	3.583
8	2.305	2.476	2.658	2.853	3.059	3.278	3.511	3.759	4.021	4.300
9	2.558	2.773	3.004	3.252	3.518	3.803	4.108	4.435	4.785	5.160
10	2.839	3.106	3.395	3.707	4.046	4.411	4.807	5.234	5.695	6.192
11	3.152	3.479	3.836	4.226	4.652	5.117	5.624	6.176	6.777	7.430
12	3.498	3.896	4.334	4.818	5.350	5.936	6.580	7.288	8.064	8.916
13	3.883	4.363	4.898	5.492	6.153	6.886	7.699	8.599	9.596	10.699
14	4.310	4.887	5.535	6.261	7.076	7.987	9.007	10.147	11.420	12.839
15	4.785	5.474	6.254	7.138	8.137	9.265	10.539	11.974	13.589	15.407
16	5.311	6.130	7.067	8.137	9.358	10.748	12.330	14.129	16.171	18.488
17	5.895	6.866	7.986	9.276	10.761	12.468	14.426	16.672	19.244	22.186
18	6.543	7.690	9.024	10.575	12.375	14.462	16.879	19.673	22.900	26.623
19	7.263	8.613	10.197	12.055	14.232	16.776	19.748	23.214	27.251	31.948
20	8.062	9.646	11.523	13.743	16.366	19.461	23.105	27.393	32.429	38.337
21	8.949	10.804	13.021	15.667	18.821	22.574	27.033	32.323	38.591	46.005
22	9.933	12.100	14.713	17.861	21.644	26.186	31.629	38.141	45.923	55.205
23	11.026	13.552	16.626	20.361	24.891	30.376	37.005	45.007	54.648	66.247
24	12.239	15.178	18.788	23.212	28.625	35.236	43.296	53.108	65.031	79.496
25	13.585	17.000	21.230	26.461	32.918	40.874	50.656	62.667	77.387	95.395
30	22.892	29.960	39.115	50.949	66.210	85.849	111.061	143.367	184.672	237.373
40	64.999	93.049	132.776	188.876	267.856	378.715	533.846	750.353	1051.642	1469.740
50	184.559	288.996	450.711	700.197	1083.619	1670.669	2566.080	3927.189	5988.730	9100.191

n	21%	22%	23%	24%	25%	26%	27%	28%	29%	30%
1	1.210	1.220	1.230	1.240	1.250	1.260	1.270	1.280	1.290	1.300
2	1.464	1.488	1.513	1.538	1.562	1.588	1.613	1.638	1.664	1.690
3	1.772	1.816	1.861	1.907	1.953	2.000	2.048	2.097	2.147	2.197
4	2.144	2.215	2.289	2.364	2.441	2.520	2.601	2.684	2.769	2.856
5	2.594	2.703	2.815	2.932	3.052	3.176	3.304	3.436	3.572	3.713
6	3.138	3.297	3.463	3.635	3.815	4.001	4.196	4.398	4.608	4.827
7	3.797	4.023	4.259	4.508	4.768	5.042	5.329	5.629	5.945	6.275
8	4.595	4.908	5.239	5.589	5.960	6.353	6.767	7.206	7.669	8.157
9	5.560	5.987	6.444	6.931	7.451	8.004	8.595	9.223	9.893	10.604
10	6.727	7.305	7.926	8.594	9.313	10.086	10.915	11.806	12.761	13.786
11	8.140	8.912	9.749	10.657	11.642	12.708	13.862	15.112	16.462	17.921
12	9.850	10.872	11.991	13.215	14.552	16.012	17.605	19.343	21.236	23.298
13	11.918	13.264	14.749	16.386	18.190	20.175	22.359	24.759	27.395	30.287
14	14.421	16.182	18.141	20.319	22.737	25.420	28.395	31.691	35.339	39.373
15	17.449	19.742	22.314	25.195	28.422	32.030	36.062	40.565	45.587	51.185
16	21.113	24.085	27.446	31.242	35.527	40.357	45.799	51.923	58.808	66.541
17	25.547	29.384	33.758	38.740	44.409	50.850	58.165	66.461	75.862	86.503
18	30.912	35.848	41.523	48.038	55.511	64.071	73.869	85.070	97.862	112.454
19	37.404	43.735	51.073	59.567	69.389	80.730	93.813	108.890	126.242	146.190
20	45.258	53.357	62.820	73.863	86.736	101.720	119.143	139.379	162.852	190.047
21	54.762	65.095	77.268	91.591	108.420	128.167	151.312	178.405	210.079	247.061
22	66.262	79.416	95.040	113.572	135.525	161.490	192.165	228.358	271.002	321.178
23	80.178	96.887	116.899	140.829	169.407	203.477	244.050	292.298	349.592	417.531
24	97.015	118.203	143.786	174.628	211.758	256.381	309.943	374.141	450.974	542.791
25	117.388	144.207	176.857	216.539	264.698	323.040	393.628	478.901	581.756	705.627
30	304.471	389.748	497.904	634.810	807.793	1025.904	1300.477	1645.488	2078.208	2619.936
40	2048.309	2846.941	3946.340	5455.797	7523.156	10346.879	14195.051	19426.418	26520.723	36117.754
50	13779.844	20795.680	31278.301	46889.207	70064.812	104354.562	154942.687	229345.875	338440.000	497910.125

n	31%	32%	33%	34%	35%	36%	37%	38%	39%	40%
1	1.310	1.320	1.330	1.340	1.350	1.360	1.370	1.380	1.390	1.400
2	1.716	1.742	1.769	1.796	1.822	1.850	1.877	1.904	1.932	1.960
3	2.248	2.300	2.353	2.406	2.460	2.515	2.571	2.628	2.686	2.744
4	2.945	3.036	3.129	3.224	3.321	3.421	3.523	3.627	3.733	3.842
5	3.858	4.007	4.162	4.320	4.484	4.653	4.826	5.005	5.189	5.378
6	5.054	5.290	5.535	5.789	6.053	6.328	6.612	6.907	7.213	7.530
7	6.621	6.983	7.361	7.758	8.172	8.605	9.058	9.531	10.025	10.541
8	8.673	9.217	9.791	10.395	11.032	11.703	12.410	13.153	13.935	14.758
9	11.362	12.166	13.022	13.930	14.894	15.917	17.001	18.151	19.370	20.661
10	14.884	16.060	17.319	18.666	20.106	21.646	23.292	25.049	26.924	28.925
11	19.498	21.199	23.034	25.012	27.144	29.439	31.910	34.567	37.425	40.495
12	25.542	27.982	30.635	33.516	36.644	40.037	43.716	47.703	52.020	56.694
13	33.460	36.937	40.745	44.912	49.469	54.451	59.892	65.830	72.308	79.371
14	43.832	49.756	54.190	60.181	66.784	74.053	82.051	90.845	100.509	111.190
15	57.420	64.358	72.073	80.643	90.158	100.712	112.410	125.366	139.707	155.567
16	75.220	84.953	95.857	108.061	121.713	136.968	154.002	173.005	194.192	217.793
17	98.539	112.138	127.490	144.802	164.312	186.277	210.983	238.747	269.927	304.911
18	129.086	148.022	169.561	194.035	221.822	253.337	289.046	329.471	375.198	426.875
19	169.102	195.389	225.517	260.006	299.459	344.537	395.993	454.669	521.525	597.625
20	221.523	257.913	299.937	348.408	404.270	468.571	542.511	627.443	724.919	836.674
21	290.196	340.446	398.916	466.867	545.764	637.256	743.240	865.871	1007.637	1171.343
22	380.156	449.388	530.558	625.601	736.781	865.668	1018.238	1194.900	1400.615	1639.878
23	498.004	593.192	705.642	838.305	994.653	1178.668	1394.986	1648.961	1946.854	2295.829
24	652.385	783.013	938.504	1123.328	1342.781	1602.988	1911.129	2275.564	2706.125	3214.158
25	854.623	1033.577	1248.210	1505.258	1812.754	2180.063	2618.245	3140.275	3761.511	4499.816
30	3297.081	4142.008	5194.516	6503.285	8128.426	10142.914	12636.086	15716.703	19517.969	24201.043
40	49072.621	66519.313	89962.188	121388.437	163433.875	219558.625	294317.937	393684.687	525508.312	700022.688

Appendix C
Present Value Interest Factor (PVIF)

Present Value of $1–$PVIF_{i\%,\, n \text{ years}}$

n	1%	2%	3%	4%	5%	6%	7%	8%	9%	10%
1	.990	.980	.971	.962	.952	.943	.935	.926	.917	.909
2	.980	.961	.943	.925	.907	.890	.873	.857	.842	.826
3	.971	.942	.915	.889	.864	.840	.816	.794	.772	.751
4	.961	.924	.888	.855	.823	.792	.763	.735	.708	.683
5	.951	.906	.863	.822	.784	.747	.713	.681	.650	.621
6	.942	.888	.837	.790	.746	.705	.666	.630	.596	.564
7	.933	.871	.813	.760	.711	.665	.623	.583	.547	.513
8	.923	.853	.789	.731	.677	.627	.582	.540	.502	.467
9	.914	.837	.766	.703	.645	.592	.544	.500	.460	.424
10	.905	.820	.744	.676	.614	.558	.508	.463	.422	.386
11	.896	.804	.722	.650	.585	.527	.475	.429	.388	.350
12	.887	.789	.701	.625	.557	.497	.444	.397	.356	.319
13	.879	.773	.681	.601	.530	.469	.415	.368	.326	.290
14	.870	.758	.661	.577	.505	.442	.388	.340	.299	.263
15	.861	.743	.642	.555	.481	.417	.362	.315	.275	.239
16	.853	.728	.623	.534	.458	.394	.339	.292	.252	.218
17	.844	.714	.605	.513	.436	.371	.317	.270	.231	.198
18	.836	.700	.587	.494	.416	.350	.296	.250	.212	.180
19	.828	.686	.570	.475	.396	.331	.277	.232	.194	.164
20	.820	.673	.554	.456	.377	.312	.258	.215	.178	.149
21	.811	.660	.538	.439	.359	.294	.242	.199	.164	.135
22	.803	.647	.522	.422	.342	.278	.226	.184	.150	.123
23	.795	.634	.507	.406	.326	.262	.211	.170	.138	.112
24	.788	.622	.492	.390	.310	.247	.197	.158	.126	.102
25	.780	.610	.478	.375	.295	.233	.184	.146	.116	.092
30	.742	.552	.412	.308	.231	.174	.131	.099	.075	.057
40	.672	.453	.307	.208	.142	.097	.067	.046	.032	.022
50	.608	.372	.228	.141	.087	.054	.034	.021	.013	.009

n	11%	12%	13%	14%	15%	16%	17%	18%	19%	20%
1	.901	.893	.885	.877	.870	.862	.855	.847	.840	.833
2	.812	.797	.783	.769	.756	.743	.731	.718	.706	.694
3	.731	.712	.693	.675	.658	.641	.624	.609	.593	.579
4	.659	.636	.613	.592	.572	.552	.534	.516	.499	.482
5	.593	.567	.543	.519	.497	.476	.456	.437	.419	.402
6	.535	.507	.480	.456	.432	.410	.390	.370	.352	.335
7	.482	.452	.425	.400	.376	.354	.333	.314	.296	.279
8	.434	.404	.376	.351	.327	.305	.285	.266	.249	.233
9	.391	.361	.333	.308	.284	.263	.243	.225	.209	.194
10	.352	.322	.295	.270	.247	.227	.208	.191	.176	.162
11	.317	.287	.261	.237	.215	.195	.178	.162	.148	.135
12	.286	.257	.231	.208	.187	.168	.152	.137	.124	.112
13	.258	.229	.204	.182	.163	.145	.130	.116	.104	.093
14	.232	.205	.181	.160	.141	.125	.111	.099	.088	.078
15	.209	.183	.160	.140	.123	.108	.095	.084	.074	.065
16	.188	.163	.141	.123	.107	.093	.081	.071	.062	.054
17	.170	.146	.125	.108	.093	.080	.069	.060	.052	.045
18	.153	.130	.111	.095	.081	.069	.059	.051	.044	.038
19	.138	.116	.098	.083	.070	.060	.051	.043	.037	.031
20	.124	.104	.087	.073	.061	.051	.043	.037	.031	.026
21	.112	.093	.077	.064	.053	.044	.037	.031	.026	.022
22	.101	.083	.068	.056	.046	.038	.032	.026	.022	.018
23	.091	.074	.060	.049	.040	.033	.027	.022	.018	.015
24	.082	.066	.053	.043	.035	.028	.023	.019	.015	.013
25	.074	.059	.047	.038	.030	.024	.020	.016	.013	.010
30	.044	.033	.026	.020	.015	.012	.009	.007	.005	.004
40	.015	.011	.008	.005	.004	.003	.002	.001	.001	.001
50	.005	.003	.002	.001	.001	.001	.000	.000	.000	.000

n	21%	22%	23%	24%	25%	26%	27%	28%	29%	30%
1	.826	.820	.813	.806	.800	.794	.787	.781	.775	.769
2	.683	.672	.661	.650	.640	.630	.620	.610	.601	.592
3	.564	.551	.537	.524	.512	.500	.488	.477	.466	.455
4	.467	.451	.437	.423	.410	.397	.384	.373	.361	.350
5	.386	.370	.355	.341	.328	.315	.303	.291	.280	.269
6	.319	.303	.289	.275	.262	.250	.238	.227	.217	.207
7	.263	.249	.235	.222	.210	.198	.188	.178	.168	.159
8	.218	.204	.191	.179	.168	.157	.148	.139	.130	.123
9	.180	.167	.155	.144	.134	.125	.116	.108	.101	.094
10	.149	.137	.126	.116	.107	.099	.092	.085	.078	.073
11	.123	.112	.103	.094	.086	.079	.072	.066	.061	.056
12	.102	.092	.083	.076	.069	.062	.057	.052	.047	.043
13	.084	.075	.068	.061	.055	.050	.045	.040	.037	.033
14	.069	.062	.055	.049	.044	.039	.035	.032	.028	.025
15	.057	.051	.045	.040	.035	.031	.028	.025	.022	.020
16	.047	.042	.036	.032	.028	.025	.022	.019	.017	.015
17	.039	.034	.030	.026	.023	.020	.017	.015	.013	.012
18	.032	.028	.024	.021	.018	.016	.014	.012	.010	.009
19	.027	.023	.020	.017	.014	.012	.011	.009	.008	.007
20	.022	.019	.016	.014	.012	.010	.008	.007	.006	.005
21	.018	.015	.013	.011	.009	.008	.007	.006	.005	.004
22	.015	.013	.011	.009	.007	.006	.005	.004	.004	.003
23	.012	.010	.009	.007	.006	.005	.004	.003	.003	.002
24	.010	.008	.007	.006	.005	.004	.003	.003	.002	.002
25	.009	.007	.006	.005	.004	.003	.003	.002	.002	.001
30	.003	.003	.002	.002	.001	.001	.001	.001	.000	.000
40	.000	.000	.000	.000	.000	.000	.000	.000	.000	.000
50	.000	.000	.000	.000	.000	.000	.000	.000	.000	.000

n	31%	32%	33%	34%	35%	36%	37%	38%	39%	40%
1	.763	.758	.752	.746	.741	.735	.730	.725	.719	.714
2	.583	.574	.565	.557	.549	.541	.533	.525	.518	.510
3	.445	.435	.425	.416	.406	.398	.389	.381	.372	.364
4	.340	.329	.320	.310	.301	.292	.284	.276	.268	.260
5	.259	.250	.240	.231	.223	.215	.207	.200	.193	.186
6	.198	.189	.181	.173	.165	.158	.151	.145	.139	.133
7	.151	.143	.136	.129	.122	.116	.110	.105	.100	.095
8	.115	.108	.102	.096	.091	.085	.081	.076	.072	.068
9	.088	.082	.077	.072	.067	.063	.059	.055	.052	.048
10	.067	.062	.058	.054	.050	.046	.043	.040	.037	.035
11	.051	.047	.043	.040	.037	.034	.031	.029	.027	.025
12	.039	.036	.033	.030	.027	.025	.023	.021	.019	.018
13	.030	.027	.025	.022	.020	.018	.017	.015	.014	.013
14	.023	.021	.018	.017	.015	.014	.012	.011	.010	.009
15	.017	.016	.014	.012	.011	.010	.009	.008	.007	.006
16	.013	.012	.010	.009	.008	.007	.006	.006	.005	.005
17	.010	.009	.008	.007	.006	.005	.005	.004	.004	.003
18	.008	.007	.006	.005	.005	.004	.003	.003	.003	.002
19	.006	.005	.004	.004	.003	.003	.003	.002	.002	.002
20	.005	.004	.003	.003	.002	.002	.002	.002	.001	.001
21	.003	.003	.003	.002	.002	.002	.001	.001	.001	.001
22	.003	.002	.002	.002	.001	.001	.001	.001	.001	.001
23	.002	.002	.001	.001	.001	.001	.001	.001	.001	.000
24	.002	.001	.001	.001	.001	.001	.001	.000	.000	.000
25	.001	.001	.001	.001	.001	.000	.000	.000	.000	.000
30	.000	.000	.000	.000	.000	.000	.000	.000	.000	.000
40	.000	.000	.000	.000	.000	.000	.000	.000	.000	.000

Appendix D

Future Value Interest Factor for Annuity (FVIFA)

Sum of an Annuity of \$1 for *n* Periods–$FVIFA_{i\%,\, n \text{ years}}$

n	1%	2%	3%	4%	5%	6%	7%	8%	9%	10%
1	1.000	1.000	1.000	1.000	1.000	1.000	1.000	1.000	1.000	1.000
2	2.010	2.020	2.030	2.040	2.050	2.060	2.070	2.080	2.090	2.100
3	3.030	3.060	3.091	3.122	3.152	3.184	3.215	3.246	3.278	3.310
4	4.060	4.122	4.184	4.246	4.310	4.375	4.440	4.506	4.573	4.641
5	5.101	5.204	5.309	5.416	5.526	5.637	5.751	5.867	5.985	6.105
6	6.152	6.308	6.468	6.633	6.802	6.975	7.153	7.336	7.523	7.716
7	7.214	7.434	7.662	7.898	8.142	8.394	8.654	8.923	9.200	9.487
8	8.286	8.583	8.892	9.214	9.549	9.897	10.260	10.637	11.028	11.436
9	9.368	9.755	10.159	10.583	11.027	11.491	11.978	12.488	13.021	13.579
10	10.462	10.950	11.464	12.006	12.578	13.181	13.816	14.487	15.193	15.937
11	11.567	12.169	12.808	13.486	14.207	14.972	15.784	16.645	17.560	18.531
12	12.682	13.412	14.192	15.026	15.917	16.870	17.888	18.977	20.141	21.384
13	13.809	14.680	15.618	16.627	17.713	18.882	20.141	21.495	22.953	24.523
14	14.947	15.974	17.086	18.292	19.598	21.015	22.550	24.215	26.019	27.975
15	16.097	17.293	18.599	20.023	21.578	23.276	25.129	27.152	29.361	31.772
16	17.258	18.639	20.157	21.824	23.657	25.672	27.888	30.324	33.003	35.949
17	18.430	20.012	21.761	23.697	25.840	28.213	30.840	33.750	36.973	40.544
18	19.614	21.412	23.414	25.645	28.132	30.905	33.999	37.450	41.301	45.599
19	20.811	22.840	25.117	27.671	30.539	33.760	37.379	41.446	46.018	51.158
20	22.019	24.297	26.870	29.778	33.066	36.785	40.995	45.762	51.159	57.274
21	23.239	25.783	28.676	31.969	35.719	39.992	44.865	50.422	56.764	64.002
22	24.471	27.299	30.536	34.248	38.505	43.392	49.005	55.456	62.872	71.402
23	25.716	28.845	32.452	36.618	41.430	46.995	53.435	60.893	69.531	79.542
24	26.973	30.421	34.426	39.082	44.501	50.815	58.176	66.764	76.789	88.496
25	28.243	32.030	36.459	41.645	47.726	54.864	63.248	73.105	84.699	98.346
30	34.784	40.567	47.575	56.084	66.438	79.057	94.459	113.282	136.305	164.491
40	48.885	60.401	75.400	95.024	120.797	154.758	199.630	295.052	337.872	442.580
50	64.461	84.577	112.794	152.664	209.341	290.325	406.516	573.756	815.051	1163.865

n	11%	12%	13%	14%	15%	16%	17%	18%	19%	20%
1	1.000	1.000	1.000	1.000	1.000	1.000	1.000	1.000	1.000	1.000
2	2.110	2.120	2.130	2.140	2.150	2.160	2.170	2.180	2.190	2.200
3	3.342	3.374	3.407	3.440	3.472	3.506	3.539	3.572	3.606	3.640
4	4.710	4.779	4.850	4.921	4.993	5.066	5.141	5.215	5.291	5.368
5	6.228	6.353	6.480	6.610	6.742	6.877	7.014	7.154	7.297	7.442
6	7.913	8.115	8.323	8.535	8.754	8.977	9.207	9.442	9.683	9.930
7	9.783	10.089	10.405	10.730	11.067	11.414	11.772	12.141	12.523	12.916
8	11.859	12.300	12.757	13.233	13.727	14.240	14.773	15.327	15.902	16.499
9	14.164	14.776	15.416	16.085	16.786	17.518	18.285	19.086	19.923	20.799
10	16.722	17.549	18.420	19.337	20.304	21.321	22.393	23.521	24.709	25.959
11	19.561	20.655	21.814	23.044	24.349	25.733	27.200	28.755	30.403	32.150
12	22.713	24.133	25.650	27.271	29.001	30.850	32.824	34.931	37.180	39.580
13	26.211	28.029	29.984	32.088	34.352	36.786	39.404	42.218	45.244	48.496
14	30.095	32.392	34.882	37.581	40.504	43.672	47.102	50.818	54.841	59.196
15	34.405	37.280	40.417	43.842	47.580	51.659	56.109	60.965	66.260	72.035
16	39.190	42.753	46.671	50.980	55.717	60.925	66.648	72.938	79.850	87.442
17	44.500	48.883	53.738	59.117	65.075	71.673	78.978	87.067	36.021	105.930
18	50.396	55.749	61.724	68.393	75.836	84.140	93.404	103.739	115.265	128.116
19	56.939	64.439	70.748	78.968	88.211	98.603	110.283	123.412	138.165	154.739
20	64.202	72.052	80.946	91.024	102.443	115.379	130.031	146.626	165.417	186.687
21	72.264	81.698	92.468	104.767	118.809	134.840	153.136	174.019	197.846	225.024
22	81.213	92.502	105.489	120.434	137.630	157.414	180.169	206.342	236.436	271.028
23	91.147	104.602	120.203	138.295	159.274	183.600	211.798	244.483	282.359	326.234
24	102.173	118.154	136.829	158.656	184.166	213.976	248.803	289.490	337.007	392.480
25	114.412	133.333	155.616	181.867	212.790	249.212	292.099	342.598	402.038	471.976
30	199.018	241.330	293.192	356.778	434.738	530.306	647.423	790.932	966.698	1181.865
40	581.812	767.080	1013.667	1341.979	1779.048	2360.724	3134.412	4163.094	5529.711	7343.715
50	1668.723	2399.975	3459.344	4994.301	7217.488	10435.449	15088.805	21812.273	31514.492	45496.094

n	21%	22%	23%	24%	25%	26%	27%	28%	29%	30%
1	1.000	1.000	1.000	1.000	1.000	1.000	1.000	1.000	1.000	1.000
2	2.210	2.220	2.230	2.240	2.250	2.260	2.270	2.280	2.290	2.300
3	3.674	3.708	3.743	3.778	3.813	3.848	3.883	3.918	3.954	3.990
4	5.446	5.524	5.604	5.684	5.766	5.848	5.931	6.016	6.101	6.187
5	7.589	7.740	7.893	8.048	8.207	8.368	8.533	8.700	8.870	9.043
6	10.183	10.442	10.708	10.980	11.259	11.544	11.837	12.136	12.442	12.756
7	13.321	13.740	14.171	14.615	15.073	15.546	16.032	16.534	17.051	17.583
8	17.119	17.762	18.430	19.123	19.842	20.588	21.361	22.163	22.995	23.858
9	21.714	22.670	23.669	24.712	25.802	26.940	28.129	29.369	30.664	32.015
10	27.274	28.657	30.113	31.643	33.253	34.945	36.723	38.592	40.556	42.619
11	34.001	35.962	38.039	40.238	42.566	45.030	47.639	50.398	53.318	56.405
12	42.141	44.873	47.787	50.895	54.208	57.738	61.501	65.510	69.780	74.326
13	51.991	55.745	59.778	64.109	68.760	73.750	79.106	84.853	91.016	97.624
14	63.909	69.009	74.528	80.496	86.949	93.925	101.465	109.611	118.411	127.912
15	78.330	85.191	92.669	100.815	109.687	119.346	129.860	141.302	153.750	167.285
16	95.779	104.933	114.983	126.010	138.109	151.375	165.922	181.867	199.337	218.470
17	116.892	129.019	142.428	157.252	173.636	191.733	211.721	233.790	258.145	285.011
18	142.439	158.403	176.187	195.993	218.045	242.583	269.885	300.250	334.006	371.514
19	173.351	194.251	217.710	244.031	273.556	306.654	343.754	385.321	431.868	483.968
20	210.755	237.986	268.783	303.598	342.945	387.384	437.568	494.210	558.110	630.157
21	256.013	291.343	331.603	377.461	429.681	489.104	556.710	633.589	720.962	820.204
22	310.775	356.438	408.871	469.052	538.101	617.270	708.022	811.993	931.040	1067.265
23	377.038	435.854	503.911	582.624	673.626	778.760	990.187	1040.351	1202.042	1388.443
24	457.215	532.741	620.810	723.453	843.032	982.237	1144.237	1332.649	1551.634	1805.975
25	554.230	650.944	764.596	898.082	1054.791	1238.617	1454.180	1706.790	2002.608	2348.765
30	1445.111	1767.044	2160.459	2640.881	3227.172	3941.953	4812.891	5873.172	7162.785	8729.805
40	9749.141	12936.141	17153.691	22728.367	30088.621	39791.957	52570.707	69376.562	91447.375	120389.375

n	31%	32%	33%	34%	35%	36%	37%	38%	39%	40%
1	1.000	1.000	1.000	1.000	1.000	1.000	1.000	1.000	1.000	1.000
2	2.310	2.320	2.330	2.340	2.350	2.360	2.370	2.380	2.390	2.400
3	4.026	4.062	4.099	4.136	4.172	4.210	4.247	4.284	4.322	4.360
4	6.274	6.362	6.452	6.542	6.633	6.725	6.818	6.912	7.008	7.104
5	9.219	9.398	9.581	9.766	9.954	10.146	10.341	10.539	10.741	10.946
6	13.077	13.406	13.742	14.086	14.438	14.799	15.167	15.544	15.930	16.324
7	18.131	18.696	19.277	19.876	20.492	21.126	21.779	22.451	23.142	23.853
8	24.752	25.678	26.638	27.633	28.664	29.732	30.837	31.982	33.167	34.395
9	33.425	34.895	36.429	38.028	39.696	41.435	43.247	45.135	47.103	49.152
10	44.786	47.062	49.451	51.958	54.590	57.351	60.248	63.287	66.473	69.813
11	59.670	63.121	66.769	70.624	74.696	78.998	83.540	88.335	93.397	98.739
12	79.167	84.320	89.803	95.636	101.840	108.437	115.450	122.903	130.822	139.234
13	104.709	112.302	120.438	129.152	138.484	148.474	159.166	170.606	182.842	195.928
14	138.169	149.239	161.183	174.063	187.953	202.925	219.058	236.435	255.151	275.299
15	182.001	197.996	215.373	234.245	254.737	276.978	301.109	327.281	355.659	386.418
16	239.421	262.354	287.446	314.888	344.895	377.690	413.520	452.647	495.366	541.985
17	314.642	347.307	383.303	422.949	466.608	514.658	567.521	625.652	689.558	759.778
18	413.180	459.445	510.792	567.751	630.920	700.935	778.504	864.399	959.485	1064.689
19	542.266	607.467	680.354	761.786	852.741	954.271	1067.551	1193.870	1334.683	1491.563
20	711.368	802.856	905.870	1021.792	1152.200	1298.809	1463.544	1648.539	1856.208	2089.188
21	932.891	1060.769	1205.807	1370.201	1556.470	1767.380	2006.055	2275.982	2581.128	2925.862
22	1223.087	1401.215	1604.724	1837.068	2102.234	2404.636	2749.294	3141.852	3588.765	4097.203
23	1603.243	1850.603	2135.282	2462.669	2839.014	3271.304	3767.532	4336.750	4989.379	5737.078
24	2101.247	2443.795	2840.924	3300.974	3833.667	4449.969	5162.516	5985.711	6936.230	8032.906
25	2753.631	3226.808	3779.428	4424.301	5176.445	6052.957	7073.645	8261.273	9642.352	11247.062
30	10632.543	12940.672	15737.945	19124.434	23221.258	28172.016	34148.906	41357.227	50043.625	60500.207

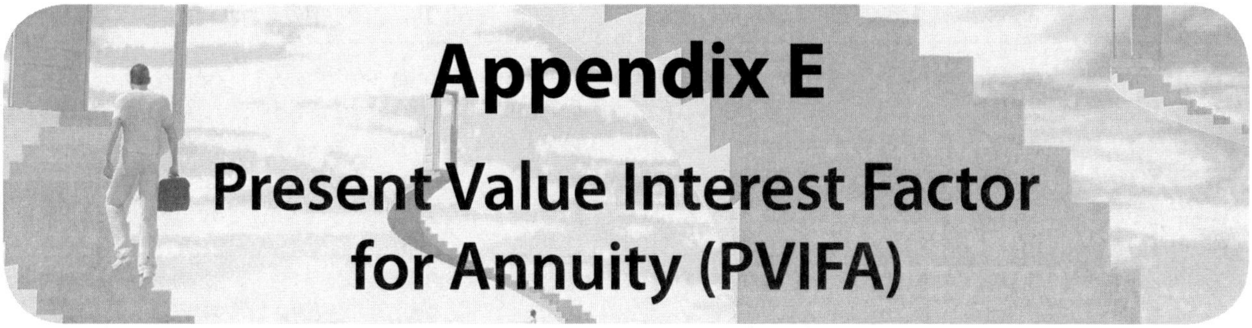

Appendix E

Present Value Interest Factor for Annuity (PVIFA)

Present Value of an Annuity of $1 for *n* Periods–$PVIFA_{i\%, n \text{ years}}$

n	1%	2%	3%	4%	5%	6%	7%	8%	9%	10%
1	.990	.980	.971	.962	.952	.943	.935	.926	.917	.909
2	1.970	1.942	1.913	1.886	1.859	1.833	1.808	1.3783	1.759	1.736
3	2.941	2.884	2.829	2.775	2.723	2.673	2.624	2.577	2.531	2.487
4	3.902	3.808	3.717	3.630	3.546	3.465	3.387	3.312	3.240	3.170
5	4.853	4.713	4.580	4.452	4.329	4.212	4.100	3.993	3.890	3.791
6	5.795	5.601	5.417	5.242	5.076	4.917	4.767	5.623	4.486	4.355
7	6.728	6.472	6.230	6.002	5.786	5.582	5.389	5.206	5.033	4.868
8	7.652	7.326	7.020	6.733	6.463	6.210	5.971	5.747	5.535	5.335
9	8.566	8.162	7.786	7.435	7.108	6.802	6.515	6.247	5.995	5.759
10	9.471	8.983	8.530	8.111	7.722	7.360	7.024	6.710	6.418	6.145
11	10.368	9.787	9.253	8.760	8.306	7.887	7.499	7.139	6.805	6.495
12	11.255	10.575	9.954	9.385	8.863	8.384	7.943	7.536	7.161	6.814
13	12.134	11.348	10.635	9.986	9.394	8.853	8.358	7.904	7.487	7.103
14	13.004	12.106	11.296	10.563	9.899	9.295	8.746	8.244	7.786	7.367
15	13.865	12.849	11.938	11.118	10.380	9.712	9.108	8.560	8.061	7.606
16	14.718	13.578	12.561	11.652	10.838	10.106	9.447	8.851	8.313	7.824
17	15.562	14.292	13.166	12.166	11.274	10.477	9.763	9.122	8.544	8.022
18	16.398	14.992	13.754	12.659	11.690	10.828	10.059	9.372	8.756	8.201
19	17.226	15.679	14.324	13.134	12.085	11.158	10.336	9.604	8.950	8.365
20	18.046	16.352	14.878	13.590	12.462	11.470	10.594	9.818	9.129	8.514
21	18.857	17.011	15.415	14.029	12.821	11.764	10.836	10.017	9.292	8.649
22	19.661	17.658	15.937	14.451	13.163	12.042	11.061	10.201	9.442	8.772
23	20.456	18.292	16.444	14.857	13.489	12.303	11.272	10.371	9.580	8.883
24	21.244	18.914	16.936	15.247	13.799	12.550	11.469	10.529	9.707	8.985
25	22.023	19.524	17.413	15.622	14.094	12.783	11.654	10.675	9.823	9.077
30	25.808	22.397	19.601	17.292	15.373	13.765	12.409	11.258	10.274	9.427
40	32.835	27.356	23.115	19.793	17.159	15.046	13.332	11.925	10.757	9.779
50	39.197	31.424	25.730	21.482	18.256	15.762	13.801	12.234	10.962	9.915

n	11%	12%	13%	14%	15%	16%	17%	18%	19%	20%
1	.901	.893	.885	.877	.870	.862	.855	.847	.840	.833
2	1.713	1.690	1.668	1.647	1.626	1.605	1.585	1.566	1.547	1.528
3	2.444	2.402	2.361	2.322	2.283	2.246	2.210	2.174	2.140	2.106
4	3.102	3.037	2.974	2.914	2.855	2.798	2.743	2.690	2.639	2.589
5	3.696	3.605	3.517	3.433	3.352	3.274	3.199	3.127	3.058	2.991
6	4.231	4.111	3.998	3.889	3.784	3.685	3.589	3.498	3.410	3.326
7	4.712	4.564	4.423	4.288	4.160	4.039	3.922	3.812	3.706	3.605
8	5.146	4.968	4.799	4.639	4.487	4.344	4.207	4.078	3.954	3.837
9	5.537	5.328	5.132	4.946	4.772	4.607	4.451	4.303	4.163	4.031
10	5.889	5.650	5.246	5.216	5.019	4.833	4.659	4.494	4.339	4.192
11	6.207	5.938	5.687	5.453	5.234	5.029	4.836	4.656	4.487	4.327
12	6.492	6.194	5.918	5.660	5.421	5.197	4.988	4.793	4.611	4.439
13	6.750	6.424	6.122	5.842	5.583	5.342	5.118	4.910	4.715	4.533
14	6.982	6.628	6.303	6.002	5.724	5.468	5.229	5.008	4.802	4.611
15	7.191	6.811	6.462	6.142	5.847	5.575	5.324	5.092	4.876	4.675
16	7.379	6.974	6.604	6.265	5.954	5.669	5.405	5.162	4.938	4.730
17	7.549	7.120	6.729	6.373	6.047	5.749	5.475	5.222	4.990	4.775
18	7.702	7.250	6.840	6.467	6.128	5.818	5.534	5.273	5.033	4.812
19	7.839	7.366	6.938	6.550	6.198	5.877	5.585	5.316	5.070	4.843
20	7.963	7.469	7.025	6.623	6.259	5.929	5.628	5.353	5.101	4.870
21	8.075	7.562	7.102	6.687	6.312	5.973	5.665	5.384	5.127	4.891
22	8.176	7.645	7.170	6.743	6.359	6.011	5.696	5.410	5.149	4.909
23	8.266	7.718	7.230	6.792	6.399	6.044	5.723	5.432	5.167	4.925
24	8.348	7.784	7.283	6.835	6.434	6.073	5.747	5.451	5.182	4.937
25	8.422	7.843	7.330	6.873	6.464	6.097	5.766	5.467	5.195	4.948
30	8.694	8.055	7.496	7.003	6.566	6.177	5.829	5.517	5.235	4.979
40	8.951	8.244	7.634	7.105	6.642	6.233	5.871	5.548	5.258	4.997
50	9.042	8.305	7.675	7.133	6.661	6.246	5.880	5.554	5.262	4.999

n	21%	22%	23%	24%	25%	26%	27%	28%	29%	30%
1	.826	.820	.813	.806	.800	.794	.787	.781	.775	.769
2	1.509	1.492	1.474	1.457	1.440	1.424	1.407	1.392	1.376	1.361
3	2.074	2.042	2.011	1.981	1.952	1.923	1.896	1.868	1.842	1.816
4	2.540	2.494	2.448	2.404	2.362	2.320	2.280	2.241	2.203	2.166
5	2.926	2.864	2.803	2.745	2.689	2.635	2.583	2.532	2.483	2.436
6	3.245	3.167	3.092	3.020	2.951	2.885	2.821	2.759	2.700	2.643
7	3.508	3.416	3.327	3.242	3.161	3.083	3.009	2.937	2.868	2.802
8	3.726	3.619	3.518	3.421	3.329	3.241	3.156	3.076	2.999	2.925
9	3.905	3.786	3.673	3.566	3.463	3.366	3.273	3.184	3.100	3.019
10	4.054	3.923	3.799	3.682	3.570	3.465	3.364	3.269	3.178	3.092
11	4.177	4.035	3.902	3.776	3.656	3.544	3.437	3.335	3.329	3.147
12	4.278	4.127	3.985	3.851	3.725	3.606	3.493	3.387	3.286	3.190
13	4.362	4.203	4.053	3.912	3.780	3.656	3.538	3.427	3.322	3.223
14	4.432	4.265	4.108	3.962	3.824	3.695	3.573	3.459	3.351	3.249
15	4.489	4.315	4.153	4.001	3.859	3.726	3.601	3.483	3.373	3.268
16	4.536	4.357	4.189	4.003	3.887	3.751	3.623	3.503	3.390	3.283
17	4.576	4.391	4.219	4.059	3.910	3.771	3.640	3.518	3.403	3.295
18	4.608	4.419	4.243	4.080	3.928	3.786	3.654	3.529	3.413	3.304
19	4.635	4.442	4.263	4.097	3.942	3.799	3.664	3.539	3.421	3.311
20	4.657	4.460	4.279	4.110	3.954	3.808	3.673	3.546	3.427	3.316
21	4.675	4.476	4.292	4.121	3.963	3.816	3.679	3.551	3.432	3.320
22	4.690	4.488	4.302	4.130	3.970	3.822	3.684	3.556	3.436	3.323
23	4.703	4.499	4.311	4.137	3.976	3.827	3.689	3.559	3.438	3.325
24	4.713	4.507	4.318	4.143	3.981	3.831	3.692	3.562	3.441	3.327
25	4.721	4.514	4.323	4.147	3.985	3.834	3.694	3.564	3.442	3.329
30	4.746	4.534	4.339	4.160	3.995	3.842	3.701	3.569	3.447	3.332
40	4.760	4.544	4.347	4.166	3.999	3.846	3.703	3.571	3.448	3.333
50	4.762	4.545	4.348	4.167	4.000	3.846	3.704	3.571	3.448	3.333

n	31%	32%	33%	34%	35%	36%	37%	38%	39%	40%
1	.763	.758	.752	.746	.741	.735	.730	.725	.719	.714
2	1.346	1.331	1.317	1.303	1.289	1.276	1.263	1.250	1.237	1.224
3	1.791	1.766	1.742	1.719	1.696	1.673	1.652	1.630	1.609	1.589
4	2.130	2.096	2.062	2.029	1.997	1.966	1.935	1.906	1.877	1.849
5	2.390	2.345	2.302	2.260	2.220	2.181	2.143	2.106	2.070	2.035
6	2.588	2.534	2.483	2.433	2.385	2.339	2.294	2.251	2.209	2.168
7	2.739	2.677	2.619	2.562	2.508	2.455	2.404	2.355	2.308	2.263
8	2.854	2.786	2.721	2.658	2.598	2.540	2.485	2.432	2.380	2.331
9	2.942	2.368	2.798	2.730	2.665	2.603	2.544	2.487	2.432	2.379
10	3.009	2.930	2.855	2.784	2.715	2.649	2.587	2.527	2.469	2.414
11	3.060	2.978	2.899	2.824	2.752	2.683	2.618	2.555	2.496	2.438
12	3.100	3.013	2.931	2.853	2.779	2.708	2.641	2.576	2.515	2.456
13	3.129	3.040	2.956	2.876	2.799	2.727	2.658	2.592	2.529	2.469
14	3.152	3.061	2.974	2.892	2.814	2.740	2.670	2.603	2.539	2.477
15	3.170	3.076	2.988	2.905	2.825	2.750	2.679	2.611	2.546	2.484
16	3.183	3.088	2.999	2.914	2.834	2.757	2.685	2.616	2.551	2.489
17	3.193	3.097	3.007	2.921	2.840	2.763	2.690	2.621	2.555	2.492
18	3.201	3.104	3.012	2.926	2.844	2.767	2.693	2.624	2.557	2.494
19	3.207	3.109	3.017	2.930	2.848	2.770	2.696	2.626	2.559	2.496
20	3.211	3.113	3.020	2.933	2.850	2.772	2.698	2.627	2.561	2.497
21	3.215	3.116	3.023	2.935	2.852	2.773	2.699	2.629	2.562	2.498
22	3.217	3.118	3.025	2.936	2.853	2.775	2.700	2.629	2.562	2.498
23	3.219	3.120	3.026	2.938	2.854	2.775	2.701	2.630	2.563	2.499
24	3.221	3.121	3.027	2.939	2.855	2.776	2.701	2.630	2.563	2.499
25	3.222	3.122	3.028	2.939	2.856	2.776	2.702	2.631	2.563	2.499
30	3.225	3.124	3.030	2.941	2.857	2.777	2.702	2.631	2.564	2.500
40	3.226	3.125	3.030	2.941	2.857	2.778	2.703	2.632	2.564	2.500
50	3.226	3.125	3.030	2.941	2.857	2.778	2.703	2.632	2.564	2.500